It Takes More than Excellence

It Takes More than Excellence

William S. Appleton, M.D.

Prentice Hall Press

New York

Copyright © 1986 William S. Appleton, M.D.

Published by Prentice Hall Press
A Division of Simon & Schuster, Inc.
Gulf+Western Building
One Gulf+Western Plaza
New York, NY 10023

PRENTICE HALL PRESS is a trademark of Simon & Schuster, Inc.

Library of Congress Cataloging-in-Publication Data

Appleton, William S.
    It takes more than excellence.

    Includes index.
    1. Success in business. 2. Organizational effec-
tiveness. 3. Psychology, Industrial. 4. Managing
your boss. I. Title.
HF5386.A64   1987   650.1   86-16940
ISBN 0-671-60025-7

Manufactured in the United States of America

10 9 8 7 6 5 4 3 2 1

First Edition

To Amy, Lucy, Bill, and Sam—my children
To Lindy—my wife and friend
To Morris and Harriet—my parents
And finally to those who taught me about more than
  excellence—my teachers, friends, and patients

Contents

Preface

The skills I bring to this book are those of coach rather than participant. My expertise is that of a psychiatrist with a deep interest in practical results rather than theory. This has caused me to draw from a variety of psychiatric and psychological schools, business and negotiating viewpoints, and twenty-five years of clinical practice with hundreds of men and women in corporations. Nine years of writing "The Analyst's Couch" for *Cosmopolitan* magazine have helped me sharpen a capacity lacking in many doctors and psychiatrists: the ability to give clear and concise answers to people's questions. A further influence away from the ethereal toward the practical came from Dr. Elvin Semrad, who in my first year of Harvard Psychiatric training recommended that no books be read and that in their place one listen to the patient. Although I have read many volumes since, during my many years as a member of the Harvard Medical School faculty I have always retained this practical orientation.

Having listened to hundreds of working people who have been fired and passed over for promotions, and who have failed to advance in their careers, as well as those who have been extremely successful, I have been able to formulate a plan for advancement that can work for anyone. This requires adequate, sound self-esteem, knowing how to evaluate and handle your superiors, being forceful and effective in your dealings with them, and mastery of your emotions. Each of these subjects is covered in a section.

The title *It Takes More than Excellence* is not intended to belittle excellence but to try to help people learn what it takes to get ahead. I have seen too many people fail not because of their performance in the workplace but because of their weakness in the sphere of human relations. Many superior people fail to rise up the corporate ladder because they are not able to advertise their accomplishments or because they have misread their boss's psychological makeup. To get ahead you have to be good, and you have to be able to win the approval of your superiors in such a way that they recognize your strengths and *want* you to succeed. To reach your goal you need to do your job well, have the confidence to present yourself effectively, and deal skillfully with the complexity of human reactions around you.

Excellence goes unrewarded unless you combine it with the capacity to manage yourself and your boss effectively. The jungle out there is really a psychological one, and I hope my insights and advice will help many excellent people get the raises and promotions they deserve.

Self-Esteem

Why begin a book on career success with a discussion of self-esteem? Because getting ahead requires risk, creativity, and the ability to handle yourself and those around you. All of these cause anxiety and threaten your emotional security. Those who must be comfortable and have no reserve of confidence can take no chances. They do their humdrum tasks and rush home each night. But to participate on the front lines of your organization means feeling tested and often afraid. "Will this new product I have been championing really work once developed, and if so, will it sell? My career depends on it." To try what you have never before attempted and what you feel inadequately prepared to do calls for self-confidence. There is no time to get special training or study the situation at leisure; a decision must be made immediately on the basis of scanty data. What is needed is courage.

Where does this bravery come from? It derives from your sense of yourself as someone who has won in the past and has a good chance of doing so in the future. It is, in short, your self-esteem.

Self-esteem is a measure of the reputation you have with yourself. It gives you the confidence and strength to cope with the unknown when you are afraid. It is the feeling that you are both competent and worthwhile. If your self-esteem is low, you would not give yourself a raise or promotion. And if you would not, then don't expect your boss to recommend you for a leadership position. Do you feel good about yourself, worthy of more money and a part of the good life, or destined to be deprived?

You need to recognize the negative effect of low self-esteem before you will be able to overcome it. Unrecognized low self-worth can result in harm to your image at work. You will appear dependent and indecisive, afraid to say what you think and feel because you don't respect your own mind. Not many people, however, can live with the feeling that "I am stupid and my analysis of problems is faulty," and so they find effective ways to hide this painful self-appraisal. They automatically avoid challenges and responsibility, doing the minimum job and trying to get by with charm or by dragging out routine duties to fill the time, thus avoiding the challenge of the new.

Low self-esteem, therefore, can become a subtle eroder of your career. It destroys your vigor and dooms you to act in routine and safe ways. No one will give you more than the most token raise or promotion for this kind of performance. But high self-esteem will allow you to trust your abilities and use them effectively. It will enable you to stretch them and get more out of yourself.

High self-esteem must be distinguished from unrealistic euphoria. Pete Rose knows he doesn't have Ty Cobb's natural abilities, but he stretched himself to equal his hit record nonetheless. You don't have to convince yourself that you can do anything at work, only that you can get the most from your strengths and minimize your limitations. You cannot perform tasks completely beyond you just because you believe in yourself and follow some magic formula, but you can get much more out of your abilities if they have not been crushed by low self-esteem.

What Kind of Self-Esteem Do You Have?

Children's Self-Esteem

As we grow from children into adults, our sense of self changes. The young child normally inflates his or her qualities unrealistically in response to the enthusiastic encouragement of family and teachers. Without this overestimation small children would not dare to attempt new things. They learn to play the piano or catch a fly ball, try to ride a two-wheeler or take ballet lessons. Their efforts are not judged by realistic adult standards. Kids imagine they're major-leaguers or rock stars; children's self-esteem is normally unrealistically inflated. It provides the strength through fantasy and dreams for them to attempt difficult tasks and to be comforted when they fail.

The self-esteem of some people recalls too much of this childish quality, resting on fantasy rather than a true appraisal of personal strengths and weaknesses. This results in avoidance and fearfulness, a concern that the bubble of exalted feeling will be punctured by failure and rejection. It can mean doing the details of a job well and never trying to reach past the routine, because confronting personal limitations is too painful. The immature adult wards off disappointment and becomes less and less able to bear it. Anyone feels bad when failing to triumph over newly acquired responsibilities, but most people should be able to tolerate the pain, comforted by past successes. The childlike adult has little or no experience with realistic success and failure, and becomes overwhelmed. By avoiding the test, he or she tries to hide from reality and to continue the fantasy of being a star.

Sooner or later the self-deception crumbles. Others are promoted, receive raises and bonuses, move to better houses, drive nicer cars, and enjoy exotic vacations, with increasing responsibility and pleasure in their growing competence and influence. The childlike one feels neglected, unrewarded, more and more resentful. The fantasy props of self-esteem are overwhelmed by the reality of a meager living standard and failure to achieve. The childlike worker needs constant encouragement and reward, but does not have the confidence to earn the recognition so desperately craved.

Adolescent Self-Esteem and the Middle Manager

While employees with childlike self-esteem usually cannot succeed unless they mature, those who are stuck in adolescence may get ahead initially only to run into great difficulty later. Normally, the teenager has to replace the unconditional love and encouragement of parents in childhood with the more realistic criticism of teachers, peers, and family. But the transition can be painful. Self-esteem in adolescence is not the mature independent regulator that insulates from pain during difficult times. Instead, it is attached to peers. The opinions of a best friend and the clique replace those of the parents. Alas, the judgments of peers and teachers can be harsh. In addition, parents begin to expect not only more but different behavior from that fostered by the peer group. The result is a sharp fall in self-esteem, from the fantasy-based one of childhood to the reality-grounded one of adolescence. The anxious, angry, and depressed moods of teenagers can be attributed to low self-esteem. Clinging to best friends and conforming to a peer group are attempts to overcome these bad feelings.

The adolescent bases self-esteem more on people than on facts, so that reality is that which is confirmed by others. It is dependent on the expectations and values of others and on winning the group's approval. The decrease in anxiety that results when the approval of others is won is the teenager's substitute for true self-esteem.

If self-esteem never progresses beyond the adolescent type, a lifelong dependence on approval results. Always living according to the direction of the crowd, people with this dependence lack courage and remain followers. The middle manager is in a position in the organization comparable in some ways to that of the adolescent in the family. He or she is alternately expected to follow obediently and to lead responsibly. Those with docile adolescent self-esteem will welcome being directed by the superior, while enjoying any opportunities to be independent. But the rebellious ones will not be comfortable following commands quietly, and the insecure ones will be unable to lead confidently. Those who are moody, inconsistent, defiant, and dependent will not get big salaries or promotions, and frequently will lose their jobs.

Adolescent types have two other prime characteristics that block their way to corporate success: they are self-centered, and they have huge emotional reactions to trivial events. Their egocentrism makes them insensitive to the needs of others and poor at skillfully handling the work environment.

Fred majored in English and took a year of graduate work in the Victorian novel at Oxford before going to business school. Although computers and numbers were not his strength, he finished in the upper third of his class. Fred was delighted with his job offer from a prestigious Wall Street investment banking firm and began there with enthusiasm. But because he was so taken with himself, he failed to notice that his manager not only did not appreciate his haughty ways and affected speech, but questioned whether he was suited for business. He seemed more interested in crafting well-turned phrases in his letters and reports than in dealing with people and crunching numbers. Rather than becoming a member of the team at the office, he seemed aloof and disdainful. Although he managed to keep his mouth shut, his attitude toward those with whom he worked and toward business itself showed. If he fancied himself an Oxford don, then why didn't he go and become one, his manager wondered. The answer, of course, was that he aspired to the six-figure salary of a partner, not the six thousand dollars of the scholar.

Narcissistic self-esteem is built on dreams of glory that cause such individuals to view events in terms of their own needs. They become upset when the boss occupies the limelight, and are not content to help, and because of this their superiors are likely to find them competitive and threatening rather than reliable and useful. Such workers are not leading candidates for promotions.

The emotional overreaction of adolescentlike workers also hurts them. Sullen when not the star, they are quick to anger. When depressed, they talk about how bad they feel in the office rather than present an image of competence and mastery. Their immature self-esteem looks to be soothed by boss and co-workers. The child's wish to be given to and made to feel better overcomes the adult's capacity to affect the environment. The *affective* state of youth has not been transcended by the *effective* one of the adult.

Adult Self-Esteem

Galileo studied astronomy in the face of the papal Inquisition, and Stravinsky heard boos from the opening-night audience, but few of us are in a position not to care at all what others think while we fashion a monumental new scientific theory or write a landmark symphony. While you or I may not be so fortunately immune to opposition as we pursue our inner calling, we have adult self-esteem if we are able to be relatively free of needing to please others. Grown-ups do not have applauding parents cheering every effort. For the worker in an entry-level job just after high school or college, there is no teacher praising an essay and taking the ideas seriously. In fact, the boss is usually not very interested in what the beginner thinks. While your professor might have found your views on Shakespeare interesting and even original, your supervisor may not care about your brilliant, unique marketing strategy.

New employees must cheer their own efforts and be able to appreciate a job well done, without needing very many rewards from others. It is perhaps unfortunate but nonetheless a way of the adult work world that the task well performed is taken for granted, while only the errors and faults are mentioned. The secretary is told of misspellings and omissions, not thanked for remembering to deliver a message. The assistant account manager is seldom praised for meeting objectives in a campaign, or the young lawyer for catching errors in contracts. We must learn to praise ourselves and to enjoy the job well done without needing too much recognition from others.

Having mastered this relative self-sufficiency (few of us can stand to be entirely ignored and never praised), there are two levels of adult self-esteem to be achieved, the second of which is much more rare but, not surprisingly, the one that produces the most significant promotions and financial rewards. The more common is that of the self-directed *conformist*. This person does not need to be reminded to get the orders processed or to service the customer's needs. That which the boss would have to direct in the immature worker the conformist does unasked. Because of this, the individual becomes valued, but the financial benefits also tend to be unexceptional. Not only are such dependable employees not given major promotions, they tend to be regarded as indispensable cogs in the corporate machine, kept on for their loyalty. In a better world the faithful self-directed servant would be amply honored, but in the corporate structure it is the person with *creative* self-esteem who wins. While nice guys don't have to finish last, it is the competent originator who triumphs.

Original does not mean disturbingly disruptive, for that would constitute a threat to the boss. Those who are too impatient and unwilling to work with and through the organization will often fail to succeed. Some high-tech corporations have recognized their need for such individuals and have managed to harness their brilliance while shielding them from the bureaucracy. One gifted physicist was allowed to arrive at work at two o'clock in the afternoon because his inventions were of such value to the company. His great difficulty in getting along with others was tolerated. But most of us do not have special skills that force acceptance from others. We must win colleagues over rather than elicit tolerance from them.

The most successful form of originality is one that does not accept the position as is, but seeks to expand it so that the boss is cajoled, guided, and even forced to view the worker differently. While the conformist pleases through loyalty, the person with creative self-esteem transforms the activity and makes co-workers and superiors view him or her in a new and impressive way. These individuals get others to *perceive* their value rather than expecting them to create it. Instead of seeking out approval, such workers gain it because of attributes they respect in themselves.

To expand one's job by trying new tasks and seeking greater responsibility makes even the most adult and secure person anxious. No one is immune to fear and tension when confronting the unknown. The creative adult faces insecurities and experiences anxiety, and patiently works at overcoming them. The child hides from fear, the adolescent conforms, and the adult conquers it.

Dressing for Success Is Not Enough

George Brett is asked his secret of hitting and says it is the feeling that "he's going downtown," that he can jump on the ball and hit it out. His secret is not the size of his bat or the cut of his uniform; it is self-esteem. Unfortunately, most of the authors of books on how to get a raise or promotion have missed Brett's point. Before you learn to negotiate, be assertive, use the right body language, and dress for success, you must believe in your ability to win. Your conviction that you will succeed must be present not just on the fateful day you face your boss with your request but long before, in the way you handle yourself, your job, and the people with whom you come in contact. If you do not think you are a winner, a knowledgeable person with whom to be reckoned, then wearing expensive suits or designer dresses will not guarantee your success. Nor will long practice sessions on how to talk to your superior on the day you ask for your promotion and salary increase. You may look right and say the correct words, but you must have confidence to inspire it in others. High morale means you believe in yourself, your company, and its products, that you have the conviction that customers would be well served if they bought from you and that your boss's interests would be helped if he or she listened to you. While you need social skills to communicate your good feeling about yourself to those around you, you must have confidence before you can exude it.

Normal Fear in Seeking Success

It is normal for your self-esteem to be threatened when you ask for a raise or promotion, for two reasons: fear of judgment and fear of abandonment. Seeking advancement exposes you to the scrutiny of those who know you well. To be refused is to be told in some sense that your superior does not value you highly, no matter how euphemistically the rejection is couched. And it also subjects you to the fear of abandonment, that you will be fired or forced to quit. Solid self-esteem does not make anyone immune to fear; the danger of harsh judgment or abandonment upsets the most secure person. But the creative adult uses mature psychological defenses to counter this stress.

Avoiding the anxiety of seeking a raise or promotion is so common that it became a familiar scene in old movies to have the wife encourage the husband to go in and stand up to his boss for a fair salary. It is surprising to me how many people never push to get ahead and how skillful they are at skirting the whole issue, often without realizing it. "My company reviews salaries once a year and calls you in at that time." This acceptance of company policy relieves the employee of all need for initiative. "My boss can't give me a raise now because he'd have to give everyone a raise and that's impossible." There are those who love their jobs and are uninterested in money, despite the fact that they do not have enough to pay their bills or live comfortably. In accepting the status quo and not thinking about improving their financial status, these individuals are in fact protecting their self-esteem from the twin threats of judgment and abandonment. While they succeed in remaining relaxed, they do so as obedient children and not as creative adults.

Unconscious Guilt over Coasting

A natural tendency to coast is often responsible for the acceptance of career stagnation rather than success. There is an unconscious truce with the boss: "You let me have it easy and I won't bother you for more money or a promotion."

A famous sociological study in a factory illustrated this widespread tendency. Workers were able to wind six large spools of wire a day if they pushed and four if they kept at it, but they settled for two and a half by unspoken convention. Employers are aware that it takes renewed motivation to increase productivity. If it were not for the natural tendency of all of us to do less than our best each day, management schemes to increase work output would never be successful. The coasting employee's guilt over not performing to high standards may be diminished by various defense mechanisms that give false psychological comfort but hurt career advancement. These include avoiding the superior and denying the importance of the project. Frequently, without realizing it, the coasting employee has decided to tolerate the status quo, wait for the annual review, and accept a cost-of-living increase.

This gap between full effort and normal productivity is responsible for the normal fear in all of us, when the boss calls us in unexpectedly, that we are going to be fired. Part of us, aware of not giving a full one hundred percent, would fire ourselves. For almost all people, the recognition that they could be trying harder makes self-esteem a little shaky. Even many rigid workaholics fill twelve- to fourteen-hour days with petty tasks and unproductive meetings in the effort to hide from themselves and others their lack of meaningful labor. The best thing is to distinguish among indolence, normal productivity, and haste without rest, to not mistake reasonable effort for slothfulness or unrealistically expect peak effort except in relatively short spurts. But if you do not approve of coasting and this makes you imagine that the boss is more likely to fire you than reward you, you must first convince yourself that you are worth promoting, that your efforts measure up to your own fair standards.

Your Childhood and Your Future

Because the work organization performs daily tasks and has a hierarchical structure, it arouses many of the same feelings toward the family that were present in childhood. People feel attached to those with whom they work, at times angry at authority figures, peers, and subordinates, sad when people leave, afraid when they are displeased, aroused when they are attractive, frustrated when they are aloof, and rejected when they say no. Our emotions are learned, and a main source of this is the family setting in which we grew. If our parents were kind and supportive, we expect our bosses to be. If we were overindulged and our wishes never denied, we may be excessively enraged when a superior refuses to give us our own way. Those who were ignored and neglected in childhood may find it hard to imagine a kind and generous superior at work.

But whatever your feelings were toward your family and are at work, asking for a raise or promotion accentuates them. It is a scary time because old childhood fears are reactivated as you risk being evaluated by those who know your performance. The deepest fear is of abandonment, of being fired and losing your attachment to your work family. Individuals who had tragic childhoods filled with deaths or long separations from loved ones, who were neglected or mistreated by their family, or who were not taught self-reliance are especially vulnerable to the fear of being fired. The possibility may be so deeply unsettling that the person has to avoid the danger at all costs, by holding on to the belief that since no raise is possible, there is no point in asking. Such a person believes that his or her job is his or her life, and cannot be risked. To some extent, however, we must all cope with this fear, no matter how secure our childhoods were. No one wants to be fired, and the very possibility gives us pause.

Those of us whose family life prepared us so that we do not need psychotherapy to help us cope with fear of abandonment can do so in several ways. First, the recognition that one can get another job (while a child cannot get another natural mother or father) will calm the irrational aspect of this terror. It is very comforting to quietly look around to see what is out there and to know where else you can go should the worst happen. Second, the knowledge of how you handle disappointment and anger helps. If you know that you will not lose control and walk out if you do not get everything you want, you will be less worried over losing your job. Bosses do not lay off employees because they want a salary increase, but because of unacceptable performance, economic conditions, or personality conflicts.

No one likes to be rejected or criticized. Asking for a raise certainly invites these reactions. This too reactivates childlike responses, since we are all brought up and socialized by being threatened with disapproval and loss of love. "No, Sam!" the mother says sharply, and the little boy looks over to see not her usual smiling and encouraging face, but one grimly set or angry. Sam looks upset and backs away from the delicate crystal glass he was about to seize and possibly break. The deeply ingrained desire for approval and fear of criticism remain in all of us, some more than others, depending on how we were raised.

Many people will not be able to stand no for an answer. Before beginning your campaign for more money, it would be wise to review in your mind how you would react to being denied. Do you imagine going berserk and in a rage saying something to irrevocably damage your relationship with your superior? Or do you fear becoming so depressed that you will be unable to stand the feeling of being so unappreciated? Here is where preparation can help your self-esteem cope with the trauma. Review what you think your own worth is. How can your superior's failure to reward you totally destroy your value? It is your own appraisal of your performance that really matters, and if he or she fails to recognize it, then perhaps you will be recognized in the future or perhaps you can find a new job in which you will be more appreciated. You are no longer a child whose whole world depends on parental approval, but an adult who deserves to be paid what you are worth.

The feelings aroused on the job can be powerful enough to reactivate childlike behaviors in an effort to cope with them. The relationship of emotion to action is very close when we are young, and the distinction can remain uncomfortably fuzzy all our lives. While we may no longer throw tantrums; cry, or attempt to hit others, our personalities can be excessively influenced by our efforts to overcome powerful feelings. We all know people whom we would describe as angry, envious, frightened, or tense, because one emotion dominates their personalities. There are six personality types that adversely influence the ability to win a raise or promotion. These individuals are not sick but have developed a way to handle their emotions that ultimately hurts their chances of getting ahead.

The Angry Child

Frances had graduated from a fine eastern university two years ago and after a year's floundering had found an excellent position in a field in which she had always yearned to work. Jobs in this creative area were scarce, and she felt she was learning a lot that would be valuable to her in the future. Initially she thought her boss kind and supportive, but soon this began to change. Frances became angry because she was not getting enough direction, because she was being ordered about arbitrarily, because her superior was moody and volatile, a woman too much like her mother.

A case of transference, of the arousal of attitudes more properly belonging to the interaction of parent and child? Yes, of course! But under it all was something even more subtle. It was immature self-esteem. Frances was sure her job performance was inadequate. As a beginner, she initially believed herself extremely inventive and destined to be world-famous, but within only a few months she became painfully aware that she did not know how to do layouts and was nervous when giving a presentation and unsure of herself on the phone. She wanted Wanda, her boss, to make her feel better about herself, and became more and more enraged when this did not happen. Frances had no idea that her fury at Wanda was the result of low self-esteem and not a reaction to her moody and difficult boss.

Her professors had not helped Frances overcome her child-like fantasy-based self-esteem, because she was able to fashion brilliant papers with little effort. But in the work world steady, patient labor is required, often on ordinary tasks that do not dazzle. Wanda began to view Frances not as brilliant, but as lazy and hostile. Frances, acutely aware of her insecurity and rage, not only did not dare ask for a raise (*she* would not have rewarded an employee like herself), she became sure that she would be fired. Indeed, Wanda had threatened to fire her if Frances did not get to work on time and show more interest.

While Frances serves as an extreme illustration of a person who has high ambition and low capacity for realistic effort, her style is an exaggeration of an extremely common personality type and therefore one that can serve as a useful example. Most recent graduates come into the labor force having been encouraged in school and at home. We all have within us vestiges of childlike self-esteem, which are responsible for our youthful enthusiasm and high hopes. The real work world can seem uncaring and cold. Rather than nurturing the new worker in overcoming insecurities, the boss can appear indifferent and demanding. The manager's needs take precedence over those of the new, young worker. Teachers and parents are selfless, while authority figures seem selfish. The result of this final transition from the childhood of a student to the adulthood of a worker necessitates an adjustment of self-esteem from the world of the theoretical and possible to that of the real. All beginning workers must cope with a feeling of lost youth and idealism, which causes sadness and anger. It is the style with which these unpleasant emotions are handled that determines how the new employee is experienced by superiors and peers. Just about all new workers feel anger during this transition, at either the boss or others in the organization. The degree of the feeling and the way it is expressed markedly influence the shape a young person's career will take.

The angry component of the beginner's reactions can be expressed by coming late to work, delaying or forgetting tasks, and losing messages (technically called passive aggression). The employee appears unreliable and careless rather than angry. In fact, such an individual causes hostility in the supervisor and others who work with him or her. Some entry-level people begin to withdraw when they feel the rage and try to avoid the supervisor. While no overt fights occur, the boss does not feel supported and helped and is unlikely to be pleased by such an employee. Resistance to suggestions and directions can be another sign of anger; it is motivated by an unwillingness to be "put down" by being told what to do. This is an extremely common manifestation of insecurity and low self-esteem. The newly minted worker, used to the support of family and academic life, does not want to admit the need to be shown how to do the job. A person who entertains the childlike fantasy of being a star finds the adult reality of having to learn a new task unpleasant and rejects the need. The most self-destructive form of anger is the direct expression of it toward the supervisor. This can permanently damage a career, at least in a particular organization and perhaps elsewhere, when the boss cannot recommend the employee to a new employer. An angry individual can be seen as not only unpleasant but a troublemaker who is impossible to work with. After all, a superior is looking for professional help, not the additional responsibility of a difficult child.

Techniques of anger reduction are essential for new employees. Realizing that the world of work is not school or home will help the newly hired worker tolerate emotions aroused during the transition. The understanding that it is a normal blow to self-esteem to go from brilliant and favored student to low person on the totem pole makes the experience more tolerable. Knowing that business organizations are not nearly so casual about deadlines and long lunch hours as college professors sometimes are, and that vacations are much shorter, can reduce rage. Finally, the new worker must learn to control hostility and not act on it in even the most subtle way, to go toward the supervisor in an attempt to be helpful rather than angrily avoiding interaction.

Wrath need not be expressed, especially the ire that is fueled by shaky self-esteem and that is thus inappropriate to the actual relationship between employer and employee. Anger is an emotion that involves blame and vengeance; the boss is a convenient target, often an innocent one. Before attacking, check your self-esteem. If it is low, then adjust your expectations to realistic levels, accept your imperfections, and begin a campaign to improve so that you conform to your own standards. If you still have reason to have it out with your manager, then do it when you are calm and sure that the issues are real.

The Good Child

Barbara has kept the books of her company for thirteen years, and Mr. Plimpton has been her boss all along. Until recently she was proud that he liked her and treated her with courtesy and kindness. But lately she has become increasingly upset watching younger employees win promotions and raises. She wants appreciation in the form of money and a new job title, not civil greetings. She is unaware of the childlike basis of her self-esteem and expects to be made to feel good by her boss's recognition of her loyalty and meticulous work. Unlike Frances, whose immaturity took the form of anticipating stardom with little effort, and who thus felt resentment and anger, Barbara was upset that her diligent industry and goodness were not being rewarded. Rather than having the confidence to take on new responsibilities and expand her usefulness to the company, she had perfected her tiny area. Mr. Plimpton liked his honest, hard-working bookkeeper, but he also took her for granted. He did not consider her for promotion to executive rank, with a corresponding raise in salary.

The good child is not a creative leader who finds new business for the company and takes on increasingly challenging tasks. Often he or she understands and faithfully performs a routine, sometimes complicated, procedure that no one else can do or would do. The boss may wonder how anyone else will ever be able to manage the supermarket or supervise the construction site so efficiently, but that gives no incentive to advance this person up the ladder. The best way to get a raise is to do the drone parts of your job well, or even to delegate them, while taking on the executive-type tasks, expanding sales, and widening your sphere of influence. The good child may, after long years, advance the many small steps to a vice-presidency of a bank or insurance company because of seniority and loyal service but will never make alot of money or win important leadership posts. In business, virtue is not generously rewarded; shrewdness and toughness are. It is not what you have already accomplished so much as the promise of what you will do for your superior that makes him or her want to advance you and expand your paycheck.

The Envious Child

Richard grew up in a close-knit family in a modest section of Cleveland. For thirty years his father managed the same electrical supply house, which paid him well but not exceptionally. Richard was very bright. He went to Yale and Stanford Business School. Then he began working for a large paper company, and in two years became convinced that he was destined neither for top management nor for significant remuneration. Why? Because he envied what he perceived to be the advantages of others in the organization. They had had more successful fathers who gave them confidence and the know-how to advance themselves. They could make fluent rapid-fire presentations and did not tense up. They had a large network of friends and professional contacts, sources of business sales and opportunities for changes to better jobs. Richard was certain that his advantaged colleagues had gotten their impossible-to-beat head starts in childhood, in their private schools (his was public), on the playing fields (he was nonathletic), and from their parent's contacts and in their country clubs. He envied them.

Richard felt barred from the good things of life, unable to participate in the social and human side of his company. He was uncomfortable on trips with his boss and unsure of what to say to colleagues or clients at lunch. Whenever he was not invited to a closed meeting or a sales conference, he took it as evidence that he would never be included and that his career was finished. If he made a mistake or his boss gave him a suggestion, he became even more discouraged.

Richard was very bright, and his family worshipped him throughout his childhood. The childlike fantasy basis of his self-esteem flourished. He and his parents were convinced he was something special. His admission to Yale confirmed their dream. Richard did not need to consider getting along with or competing with others. He worked hard, remained solitary, and did well. In a way, he was right about his present plight. While his colleagues were playing ball, going to dances, and learning to socialize, he was living out his self-centered childish fantasy of being better than they and special. Now his balloon was being burst. Perceiving their advantage could have been a first step in motivating him to catch up, but instead he gave up and felt depressed.

Richard had an extra dose of envy, but some amount of it is normal. Others have a happy family life, better education, greater natural intelligence, more money, and more pleasing personalities, or are better-looking or favored by the boss. But the more you allow yourself to feel that you are excluded and do not have an equal chance, the more defeated or angry you will become, and therefore the less able to enter the inner circle.

It is natural for any child to feel shut out from parental intimacy and the power and freedom of those who are older. This reaction is rekindled in the corporate hierarchy as one is not invited to certain closed meetings or to client dinners or special events. When these emotions solidify and the employee becomes reconciled to not getting what he or she wants, the possibility of promotions and raises diminishes.

A child may be born into a poor family. It is amazing how many adults continue to accept the lack of money as reality, rather than seeing it for what it represents, the extension of an early emotion into adulthood. Money and the good life are not just for others, for the lucky few born to aristocratic families. It can be yours, but only if you convince yourself that it is possible. Knowing your weaknesses is the first step to achieving adult self-esteem, rather than the imagined glory of the child, and this knowledge can be painful. Others are ahead of you in some ways—brighter, more self-assured, with better social connections—but you can build yourself up to maximize your strengths and diminish your weaknesses. This does not happen through resignation and self-pity, but through hard work.

The Guilty Child

Guilt is so widespread and subtle that it is better to survey some common examples of it than to pick out one particular type. Guilt is the strong, perhaps vague, feeling that one has done something wrong and will be punished. Real or imagined, it is why many employees worry when the boss calls them in unexpectedly or writes them a letter. One man delayed opening his mail for days, only to find not the pink slip he feared, but a bonus check.

Workers are guilty for almost as many reasons as there are people. In general it is because they have done or failed to do something their conscience dictates. The infraction may be job-related or displaced from their private lives. *Mea culpa.* Whatever the cause, the feeling becomes focused on the boss, especially when he or she calls the employee in unexpectedly or for a job review. "I have not been doing my job well enough, and my supervisor will tell me so."

If raise in salary is reward, the lack of one is the just desert of the guilty. They do not seek confrontations with their superiors over money but avoid them for fear of being denounced, even fired. Guilty people fail in their own eyes and believe their job performance substandard, worthy of punishment, not more money.

Before you assume that guilty persons are "them" and not you, think a minute. Do you believe you've been coasting on the job, with your mind distracted by your private life or filled with anger at your organization? Angry individuals expect retribution, not raises. Employees who have been taking it easy and not meeting their own standards avoid evaluation. They feel they are getting more than they deserve, rather than less.

To get promotions and more money, you must act the part

first and regard yourself as valuable, not a slacker or a malcontent. If you no longer try hard at work, ask yourself why. Do you feel bored and defeated? Is this feeling a carry-over from childhood or is it based on the reality of your job situation? Why aren't you working up to your own standard? If the job is hopeless, find a new one. Perhaps it isn't, but because you felt emotional and excluded, you became resigned and apathetic, and now you no longer try hard. Your current lack of effort makes you guilty, and your guilt keeps you from money and recognition. You remain the excluded, defeated child, guilty of short periods of inattention. Look at your overall performance, and lower your standards if they are too high.

To overcome guilt, you must live up to your own standards first and then present the results of your positive evaluation to your supervisors. Stop coasting and doing a mediocre job, or being angry and doing a bad one. Stop letting yourself and your boss down. If your present situation is hopeless, change it, but before going to the trouble of looking for a new job, give this one the full try. Healthy, creative adult self-esteem is not based on the guilty feeling of not living up to a standard and deserving punishment. Healthy adult self-esteem requires meeting your own criterion for excellence. Only then is it possible to persuade others of your worth.

The Holy Child

While holy children are more often women than men, they come in both sexes. Margaret was one. Her feelings of pride and love kept her from getting anywhere, as did her view of poverty. Margaret's values were religious, not material, and her reward was to be in the next life. She loved her boss and the company for which she worked. Aside from not promoting her or raising her salary, her boss treated her very well. He never forgot her on her birthday or at Christmas, and was appreciative and grateful for her loyal, meticulous efforts. Margaret's pride in her own job extended to the whole company. "We give the best service and our customers are satisfied," she would say.

Nonmoney values can stop promotions and raises. There were no rich saints. The dollar is equated with evil by some people. If your values are such that your self-esteem would suffer from success and wealth, then it probably is wise to remain poor. The antipleasure aspect of the Puritan ethic makes the sparse life the norm and money the instrument of the devil.

A person who works only for money and has no interest in the quality of the product, its social value, or his or her fellow workers possesses a kind of greed bordering on the monstrous. But one who cannot enjoy the fruits of labor and lives in poverty is equally askew. While we may think that Margaret, the holy child, is one of them and not us, in my experience many workers have very odd feelings about money and raises. They consider it wrong to threaten the equilibrium of boss and organization by asking for a significant raise. The fact that their superiors and the stockholders are reaping lavish rewards seems to barely stir them. The religious values deeply ingrained all their lives win out. Pride in work, loyalty to the organization, and their nonmaterial values block or at least significantly hamper their efforts to improve their financial standing.

Most of us are not MBAs who view our "net worth" as a dispassionate figure to be expanded. To some extent that is healthy, and also fortunate for the economy. One analysis of American business's inability to successfully compete with Japan, for example, attributes it to a lack of company pride and loyalty and too much focus by ruthless and narcissistic MBAs on their own career and net worth. Perhaps such caricatured materialists are reacting against holy child qualities instilled in them by their parents.

In any event, it would be useful to examine your own values regarding the mercenary and the nonmaterial. Why do you find it so hard to envision yourself financially comfortable, living in the best neighborhood, wearing fine clothes, staying in first-class hotels, and enjoying elaborate vacations? Must you live from hand to mouth? Is your self-esteem based on nonmaterial values and ultimately on economic insufficiency? Have you taken a vow of poverty?

The sense of self—how we see what we are about in the world—strongly influences our work lives. If we are holy children, strongly committed to being meek, turning the other cheek, and being loyal and obedient, we will not be rewarded in this life, at least not financially. But even if we are not one of these extreme religious characters, but retain significant teachings and values of this kind from childhood, our advance may be slowed, perhaps without our realizing it.

The Loyal Child

Michael manages a restaurant. His eyes are everywhere. On the waitress's behavior toward customers and on the speed of the cooks, the stock of food, the bartender's actions, and the stack of dirty dishes. He enforces the dress of the employees, and makes sure that they wear badges and that they do not loaf or give free drinks to their friends. He monitors receipts and seeks to maximize efficiency. But most of the time Michael seethes, because he believes his supervisors do not appreciate his ceaseless efforts. He wants their support; he wants them to be as tough on the employees as he is.

For the sixty-hour week he works—on his feet and diligent—Michael's salary is such that he cannot pay his bills. His raises are a token 4 or 5 percent a year. Yet in spite of his debts, his inability to afford a vacation or a car that works reliably, what he wants is his boss's approval. He cannot imagine leaving his job and is emotionally attached to the staff and customers of his restaurant.

Michael has no money and seems not to care. Rather than salary raises, what he wants is recognition for his effort and support for the standards he attempts to impose. His aggression comes out not because of money, but because a waitress is lazy or because his boss does not hire others to take some of the load off him. A woman he recently dated steadily made fun of him for being thirty-three years old with a rusting car, a shabby apartment, and nothing to show for his labors. Her words upset him, but he accepted the end of their affair calmly. His real attachment had never been to her anyway, but to his work family.

Few of us are as devoted to our jobs as Michael, but many were brought up to value commitment and obligation. Being a faithful employee means not deserting your boss or fellow workers, and caring about standards and the completion of projects. The pursuit of a raise may seem selfish, especially when it implies a willingness to leave the job if your need is not met. The loyal child's self-esteem prevents him or her from obtaining a raise, since the attempt to engineer one can feel dishonest and make the venture a guilty one. It can be successfully argued that a lack of interest in money is noble, not childish, and if you are a person who feels above the scrambling of the marketplace, then so long as your status doesn't cause you pain or make you angry, you may be able to persuade yourself to feel good about not getting a raise. It is hard to remain noble, however, while those of lesser moral fiber are rewarded with money and the good things it can buy.

Prosperous Self-Esteem

Your self-esteem may be solid and help you effectively do your job, yet stand in the way of your getting a raise. In spite of being mature, you may be reluctant to appear interested in money. In fact, we are all brought up not to trust the money-oriented doctor, lawyer, or clergyman. All of us would like to be recognized for the quality of our work, while receiving ample financial reward as a by-product of our excellence. Going after money directly can feel dirty and represent a threat to self-esteem.

The pure view of youth must be modified. The transformation is not from the ideal of making the world a better place to the cynicism of grabbing all one can, but from amateur to professional, from doing a good job simply for its own sake to excellence *and* financial reward. Prosperous self-esteem does not regard full payment as selling out. There is nothing wrong with the artist's work just because someone is willing to buy it for a lot of money. Being rich is not evidence of low standards. Picasso was a millionaire, and so was Giuseppe Verdi.

Those who remain idealistically aloof from money do not have to become bitter, but they frequently do, because of feeling powerless; they are angry at being denied good housing and vacations, at being unable to send their children to the best schools or drive a decent car. Sooner or later almost all but the most ascetic are forced by inflation, high rents, and the expense of food and clothing to seek more money just to maintain a standard of living, let alone improve it. But as the recognition of the need for a greater salary grows, the previously pure often feel ill-equipped to go after it. Not only are they afraid that the boss will judge them harshly or fire them, they also suffer their own ill opinion. No longer do they feel above others in their dedication to excellence rather than the almighty dollar. No different from the used-car salesman, they too are out to make a living and must calculate (often coldly) how to improve their material position. Once they have decided to do so, they may make a furtive effort, only to sink back into the belief that they are just no good with money. They may revert to a feeling of being morally superior, not one of those who can do battle in the marketplace. "I just don't have a head for money," they say, as they struggle to maintain their haughtiness and to salvage their self-esteem after their failure to get a raise or promotion.

The individual with prosperous self-esteem does not shrink so quickly from the test of winning financial reward. Such people do not allow themselves to be paid in prestige instead of money. It may be great to have a Harvard affiliation or work for the museum or symphony or write books that no one reads, but it doesn't pay the rent. Making the adjustment from youthful purity to comfortable professionalism, and learning to respect oneself for it, the prosperous adult goes after what he or she wants. Not waiting to be unafraid when confronting a superior for more money, or being above it all, such a person learns to conquer fear and to act, even when nervous.

Organizations remind you of your childhood. They are hierarchical and awe-inspiring, and arouse feelings of fear and powerlessness that activate old insecurities. The person with prosperous self-esteem replaces the *affective* (emotionally reactive) state of childhood with the *effective* capacities of the mature adult. To do this:

1. **Draw up a list of your accomplishments.** This exercise will force you to recognize your value, rather than feel defeated. Write down your weaknesses as well, and go to work eliminating them.

2. **Persuade yourself of your worth.** If you do not believe that you are doing your job well, stop and consider whether this represents irrational guilt, a severe self-imposed standard that you can never meet, or rational censure because you no longer try hard enough or pay full attention to your efforts. Why don't you push any longer? Are you angry because you feel unrewarded and unappreciated? Failing to do your best makes you unable to experience self-worth and thus to persuade others of your value, which makes them continue to not appreciate you. The result is a vicious circle of lack of effort, lack of reward, lack of effort.

3. **Be active not passive.** Once you've satisfied yourself that you deserve a raise, convince the boss. This requires action in two stages. First, you must behave in such a way that an increase in salary or promotion is warranted. This means expanding your responsibilities and effectiveness. Coasting, indifference, clock watching, and sullenness do not inspire rewards. The next step is to make your needs known to your boss. You don't get anything without asking for it. Some employees resent having to go in and negotiate a salary increase, believing that it is their right to be rewarded and their superior should come to them. They feel entitled to recognition and consider the necessity for adult action to be begging.

Tom was such a man. A star athlete with a great professional future, adored by his parents and favored over their four other children. All he needed to do was quarterback his football team to victory. His parents required him to do no chores or after-school jobs, as they did his brothers and sisters. His father supervised his training program and proudly went to all the games with his mother. But now Tom is employed by a small but growing business, becoming increasingly resentful of the hard work required and his failure to be sufficiently rewarded. He refuses to ask his boss for a raise because he firmly believes it is his superior's duty to come to him. He seriously considers quitting, even though this would mean the loss of much that he has achieved. Tom is so unwilling to approach his superior and so certain that it would be demeaning that he stays home from work for weeks hoping the boss will ask him why.

People who are passive often don't recognize the condition for what it is, but hide the truth from themselves; they believe that their behavior is motivated by loyalty, pride, nonmercenary superiority, or some other justification. Tom, the football star, considers himself so good that he ought to be chased and rewarded. Some passive people, unwilling to play the success game, are unconscious of their fear of being judged or fired; they actually believe their rationalized indifference to money and position.

It is true that some people really do not care about material rewards. But they are a small minority. Most people want a high standard of living but are too afraid or guilty to pursue the goal persistently. Ask yourself why you haven't gone after money more aggressively. Are you really not interested in salary, or are you afraid deep down? In order for your self-esteem, your sense of self-worth, to help you over the hurdle of anxiety all of us experience when asking for advancement, you must recognize your true value, live up to it and feel it, persuade others of it, and then actively go after your just desert.

How to Raise Your Self-Esteem

There is a close tie between giving yourself a raise if you need one and getting a pay raise from your boss. If your morale is tenuous it can grow to depend on the status quo at the office to avoid any threats. Depressed people, for example, tend to live limited lives, avoiding the danger of failure by sticking to a predictable routine. They do their jobs and go home. So do workers who think badly of themselves and their performance, which then becomes unimaginative and unworthy of reward. The three main causes of low self-esteem are immaturity, depression and anxiety disorders, and demoralization. We have discussed immature types at length (the angry, good, envious, guilty, holy, and loyal children) and suggested ways to eliminate whichever syndrome may plague you.

Depression and Anxiety Disorders

While this is not a study of depression but of how to get a promotion and a raise, it is necessary to consider briefly how depression can hurt job performance. Acute severe depression obviously interferes with work, but the chronic low-grade unrecognized kind can subtly affect self-esteem as well as how one regards the world and the future. It can make one expect that whatever is attempted will turn out badly. The condition saps the strength, leaving little or nothing for the creativity and drive required to achieve advancement. Such people expect to be fired rather than promoted; they avoid their superiors for fear of being judged as harshly as they criticize themselves. Chronic mild depression can, over the years, so subtly color perception that the person suffering from it does not view it as a sickness but as reality. A worker feels "I will never get a raise" or "the company cannot afford it" or "my boss doesn't like me." Chronically depressed people are commonly convinced that their negative view of their work situation is reality, not a manifestation of their illness.

Other undetected psychiatric conditions can also subtly color attitudes. The chronically anxious individual is ever ready for a calamity, expecting to be fired or given a bad review by a superior. These people too may be unaware that their expectations are pathological and arise from a psychological or biological malady. They avoid seeking a raise because they are sure they will get the opposite. While anxiety and depression are the most common conditions affecting job performance and expectations, just about every other emotional disorder lowers self-esteem. The phobic expects no positive review or raise because of having avoided business trips or making presentations, and the paranoid anticipates attack and humiliation.

One way to decide whether your reluctance to try for a promotion or raise is the result of an accurate appraisal of your work performance or an underlying emotional disorder is to imagine how you would fare if you presented yourself to your spouse, children, or friends for an evaluation. If you believe everyone would be down on you, chances are you are down on yourself, and you may need help from a psychiatrist to overcome a chronic mental disorder. Then you will be able to go at your job with new vigor and get the raise you will then deep down feel you deserve.

Demoralization

Another cause of low self-esteem is demoralization—the belief that one is ineffective, hopeless, and helpless. A low opinion of oneself seems confirmed by experience. The belief that one is not equal to the exertion required to win a raise and promotion causes restriction in effort and a self-fulfilling prophecy. Not a self-starter and unable to reach goals, the demoralized person is the very opposite of one who gets promotions and raises. He or she may feel sad, hopeless, tired, pessimistic, and irritated. Such people experience a lack of interest and trouble concentrating; they cannot make decisions and avoid being tested because they are sure of failure.

Demoralization can be the residue of any emotional illness, or it can be caused by real difficulties. Chronic, unresolvable career or marital problems can leave a person feeling hopeless and incapable. Repeated business failures or being in a job unsuited to your skills can significantly damage self-confidence, as can a severely critical or angry spouse.

Do you believe others at work are winners, but not you? That they have the confidence to deal with the boss, customers, and clients that you lack? Do you perceive others as more articulate, better connected, and more sociable? Are you convinced that your sense of worthlessness is an accurate self-assessment? If so, here are some steps that will raise your self-esteem.

1. **Fight your self-defeating feelings.** If it is true that you cannot deal with customers, practice your sales pitch, study the product in greater depth, and learn to take your defeats in stride rather than as further evidence of your defectiveness. After all, no one sells every time they try. If you feel strain between you

and your superior, go to him or her and try to smooth it out. Ask for advice and guidance, or bring in a new idea. Do this repeatedly until you sense your boss beginning to respect you and seek your assistance. Fight your self-defeating feelings by converting what seems to be overwhelming tasks into small manageable ones. The sensation that others are winners, not you, must be overcome by striving for some victories of your own. Your attitude must be changed from "Others accomplish everything" to "I made a nice sale" or "The boss seemed pleased with my suggestion that each sales meeting start with a chart of last month's results."

2. **Don't worry about feeling like a phony.** You may be aware of a real weakness, such as in making presentations to a group or convincing clients to use your company's services. Once you make the decision to try hard to improve, you must be willing to tolerate feeling like an impostor. Comparisons to accomplished public speakers and super-salespersons will only make you feel worse. As you exercise a new skill you must accept criticism from yourself and your audience and tolerate disappointment. You are likely to feel out of place and odd as you practice your new sales pitch. If you catch your inner voice saying how terrible you are and how phony you sound, fight back with the notion that maybe you aren't perfect as you try this new technique, but you will improve if you keep at it and don't give up. No one makes every sale or sways every audience. Do the best you can, and ignore the perfectionistic voice inside yourself.

3. **Stop comparing.** "Why don't you study like your brother/help with the dishes like Susy does/be considerate and polite like Johnny" parents and teachers tell children. Although we didn't like these paragons we were supposed to emulate, the habit of comparing persists. "I'm no good with numbers"

(Johnny is), "I'm terrible with people" (Susy is excellent)—the process goes on at the job, and the result is that you feel inferior. The family is a hierarchy in which someone is older, better, more competent, kinder, smarter, or a finer athlete, and the only way for the little child to avoid feeling inferior is by imagining that he or she is the best, a star. The pecking order of the family becomes the hierarchy of life. As the years go by, the fantasy of stardom is replaced by an adult acceptance that it is normal for someone else to be more popular, better-looking, or brighter, but that you are still worthwhile.

Many recently graduated MBAs divide everyone they meet into winners and losers, and judge themselves by the same harsh standard. In their minds a person is intellectually, socially, and physically victorious or defeated. For those above on the ladder there is awe and envy; for those below, contempt. Young people in business are subject to terrible depressions when they are disappointed and the bubble of triumph bursts. "I am a loser," "I'm no good with people," "I'll never make partner," they moan, and become hopeless and helpless.

All of us are brought up in the family and school hierarchy, where competition is keen and it can be imagined that there is only one toy in the world and if brother got it and you didn't, nothing is left. The way to stop living at the crossroads of victory or defeat is to realize that there is enough for everybody and that our lives encompass a long season during which we win some and lose some. Hierarchical thinking must be replaced by the realization that each of us possesses a complicated array of strengths and weaknesses. You may be more able at numbers and less persuasive with people, but the organization needs both types of workers. The financial and the sales forces can do equally well. Mature, healthy self-esteem is based on enjoying one's strengths and tolerating one's faults.

4. **Overcome perfectionism.** The model child next to whom your parents found you waiting had no faults. All self-help books advise the substitution of a more lenient standard by which one can enjoy one's accomplishments rather than suffering over one's shortcomings, but it is never easy to tolerate one's faults. While the surgeon must never operate on the wrong leg or the pilot miss a landing, most workers are expected to make some errors. Merchandise goes on sale because the buyer ordered too much, law cases are not always won, and stocks go down as well as up. Too many oversupply sales, lost legal battles, and declining investments raise neither self-esteem nor salary. Each of us must decide what is too impossible a standard, what is a high level of achievement to which we should aspire, and what is slovenly.

Self-esteem is not formed by a single success or failure but gradually, through a subconscious summation of victories and defeats. The habitual way in which one deals with reality registers in the mind for good or ill, to strengthen or weaken self-esteem. We cannot escape judging ourselves and thereby estimating our fundamental worth. Self-esteem is the confidence we have in our capacity to achieve, the feeling that "I can," and it has to be earned. Since self-esteem is a summation, it is normally never in complete jeopardy from a single failure.

The perfectionist expects to know everything, to control that for which no one can be responsible, and to never make an error. A rational standard demands that you try your best, not that you never make a mistake. Self-esteem is not a gift one is given and therefore has forever, but requires effort not only to achieve but to keep. The merchant cannot coast on last year's sales, the surgeon on past perfected techniques, but all of us must strive to expand our knowledge and skills. Ongoing growth of competence is absolutely necessary for the maintenance of self-esteem. The higher the self-esteem, the higher the goals and more difficult the challenges sought.

While the individual with high self-esteem and therefore high standards of performance may strain himself or herself, the perfectionist usually cannot act at all; he or she procrastinates, then under the gun of a deadline and disaster hurriedly dashes off what frequently is an inferior effort. In Camus's *The Plague*, the would-be writer constantly rewrites the opening sentence of his novel, striving for the perfect effect. This caricature highlights the plight of the overly scrupulous individual who is afraid to submit a completed work to the judgment of others. If you suspect that you are overly fastidious and your work output is severely slowed as a result, you should overcome this lifelong habit in the following ways:

a. *Break up the task.* By dividing your project into manageable sections you will be able to assign times and meet minideadlines. Most people work effectively for an hour before requiring a short break.

b. *Move on.* While this is easier said than done, it is essential that during your time block you replace the need to be perfect with one of high standard. The writer described by Camus would have to make a deal with himself that he write five pages no matter how bad he thought his first sentence. He must not permit himself to substitute a new obsession of rewriting the first five pages endlessly instead of the first sentence, but must force himself to go on to the next five pages. This effort is not so grim as it sounds. The need for force rapidly diminishes with each subsequent five pages, replaced by the pleasure of progress.

c. *Reason with yourself.* "Why am I so sure my attempt is bad and needs to be redone? Perhaps I should take a chance that my work is not so bad and go on with it!" One graduate student kept crossing out his answers on exams, afraid that they could not possibly be correct. He realized that his grades were sharply diminished by this practice and in later examinations stopped second-guessing himself. His grades dramatically improved.

d. *Let others judge you.* You will most likely be surprised to learn that their standards are lower than your perfectionistic ones. And even if they are able to spot a mistake, so what? Most supervisors do not feel ridicule toward a subordinate when they find an error. In fact, bosses enjoy being able to add something and feel useful. Listen, thank him or her, and don't worry.

e. *Strive to be good, not perfect.* Although the overly meticulous individual may be convinced that his performance will deteriorate if he relaxes his standard, it will almost certainly improve. What was a time-wasting, fearful striving for the faultless will be replaced by realistic effort toward high standards.

Self-Esteem Is Circular

If you feel good about yourself, it shows in your work, and if your accomplishments are excellent, your morale rises. In order to raise your self-esteem, you must recognize this interaction between how you feel about yourself and your performance. Effective elevation of self-esteem is best accomplished on two fronts. One is through understanding yourself and why you are dispirited. That has been the main focus of this chapter. You now have a greater understanding of the causes of low self-esteem, from immature clinging to various types of childhood behavior to depression and demoralization.

Sometimes, though, understanding is not enough. Low self-esteem and low performance can become a vicious circle, and you may maintain that "If I felt better, I would work harder, take more chances, be more creative, and be more aggressive about demanding my raise or promotion.''

In these cases, the best approach may be less analysis and more action. The only way to feel better about yourself and your performance may be to *do* better. This will break you out of that vicious circle and into a productive and happy cycle of high productivity, high self-esteem, and high rewards.

The Boss

Concentrate on your feelings about your boss for a moment.
Isn't is amazing how intense they can get at times? Why do you
love or hate him or her so much? One reason is that you spend
more concentrated time at your job than you do with your
friends, spouse, or children. Another is your superior's power
over you. Your boss tells you what to do. Your family and
friends would not dare to do so. Being directed and ordered
about arouses childhood passions deep within us. We must stifle
our outrage. "With all my education and experience how dare
that lightweight tell me what to do! Without me he'd be lost.
He doesn't know the first thing about the marketing plan, West
Coast sales, or new products, yet he smugly gives me orders.
I'll quit and then he'll really be lost."

Your previous experience with authority figures—especially
your parents, but also siblings, peers, teachers, and other adults—
are perhaps the most important source of the intense emotions
you feel toward your superior. If they catered to you and treated
you as if you were special, and the boss who has the power to
give you the long-awaited promotion or raise does not, you will
feel deep rage. If your father was harsh and authoritarian, a
manager with similar traits can bring forth old resentments. A
considerate leader can arouse powerful feelings of love and sex-
uality in those deprived of it in their youth. The main point is
that much of the intense emotion we experience toward those
over us is not determined by the current reality of the situation
but is the result of unconscious associations.

Managing Your Feelings

The batter steps into the box, performs his ritual, takes a deep breath, and readies himself to exclude all distractions and concentrate solely on the pitch. Your efforts are completely different. You manage your strong feelings toward your boss automatically, without consciously trying. Obviously, the batter's intensity could not be sustained throughout a long workday. But being completely unaware of how you manage your strong emotions toward your boss can hurt you. It can result in unconscious behavior that sabotages your career.

Think for a moment about how you cope with your feelings toward your superior. There are two main categories into which you might fall: the cool and the hot.

Are You Really Cool?

The cool person buries emotions, sometimes so efficiently as to be unaware of them. "What do you mean, I have strong emotional reactions toward my superior?" one told me. "He's just doing his job and I'm doing mine. It's all a play, and we are the players. It's in his interest to keep overhead down and in mine to get a raise. We're both professionals." Wonderfully mature, you might think, but just because this assistant manager sounded sensible doesn't mean she was. Her anger came out at home, leaving her relationship with her boyfriend in shambles. She was convinced that he lorded it over her and looked down on her because he had gotten a job promotion and had more money. It didn't take too much pushing from me before she expressed how upset she was with her boss for caring more for his low overhead than he did for her. Her recognition that she had been fooling herself and in fact was not cool allowed her to deal much more effectively with her manager and stop abusing her lover. The result, happily, was a raise from her boss and great improvement in her private life.

A thirty-one-year-old computer programmer slaved at his screen until his eyes smarted, trying to produce perfection. After six years in his present job, he had long since abandoned hope for anything but routine raises. His company had created a special category for slaves like him, one in which he rarely came in contact with his superior. It was as though he were in solitary confinement and the food was shoved in under the door. Every so often he was handed an assignment that lasted for days or months. Otherwise he worked alone. His feelings toward his boss were similar to those one would have toward a distant planet. "He's on the management track and I'm not," he would say, as though describing a person of a different species. He neither loved nor hated nor expected anything from this creature, whose function it was to deliver assignments. How much feeling does one have for the parcel post man? This programmer did not seethe or fight with his wife. But he did have frequent bouts of depression. After all, expecting so little from life and experiencing minimal contact with those with whom he worked brought him little joy each day. Once he became aware of the root of his depression, he realized that although he still had no interest in the management track, he did want more contact with both his superior and his fellow workers. He made a point of going to lunch with them several times a week and participated more in group projects. Feeling more a part of the work family, he rarely became depressed.

If you are in the cool category, think about whether this represents a maturity of which you are proud or a defensive withdrawal from your superior. Do your emotions burst forth too strongly elsewhere in compensation? Have you attempted to rid yourself of all feeling and as a result are only half alive?

When Your Emotions Are Too Intense

Your reactions toward your boss may be hot rather than cool, in which case you almost certainly are aware of their intensity. What you might not recognize is that your superior is a convenient target for your positive and negative emotions and that some of your responses to him or her are undeserved. The psychoanalyst calls these transference, attitudes, and emotions displaced onto the boss that derive from previous figures in your life, such as your father, mother, brother, or sister. You may conceive of your leader as someone on whom you are dependent, or whom you hate, as a benign or a malevolent figure. Your superior's power to direct, reward, and punish you encourages the development in you of childlike feelings toward a parent figure. "I hate to be told what to do," one twenty-nine-year-old woman said emphatically. "My mother tried to control my every thought and action, and so did my husband." She fiercely resented the most casual suggestion from her boss.

Strong emotions are hard to hide from the superior with whom you spend so many hours. To do so successfully requires an iron will that most of us do not possess. The message usually gets across in subtle or not so delicate ways. One's maturity affects the intensity of feeling toward the supervisor and how it is expressed. The childlike worker shows reactions directly and with little guile. The adolescent-level employee is moody, rebellious, alternately and unpredictably dependent and independent. But even the most mature worker has difficulty controlling extremes of love and hate toward the boss, because strong emotions are naturally accompanied by action. The grown-up may not attack the employer, but extreme hatred usually seeps out in avoidance, a gesture, a tense meeting, an awkward lunch. Understanding displaced transference and recognizing lingering immaturities allow the employee to calm his or her furies and deal with the boss in a rational way. Anger at the leader is by no means always neurotic, but you can more vigorously correct real injustice if you are sure that phantoms are not interfering. The rest of this chapter will help you identify and calm powerful emotions so that you can be mature in your corporate climb.

Transference as Prejudice

A prejudice is a preconceived opinion that is usually directed toward a racial, religious, or national group. Although the more newsworthy ones are hostile, prejudices can also be positive. "I like the French" is as much a bias as "I hate the French." A transference can be thought of as a personal prejudice, one you have built up as a result of your experience. "I am a leg man." "I love dark-haired men." "Tall men excite me." "I love blondes." These harmless inclinations strongly influence how we choose our mates. As Professor Henry Higgins in *My Fair Lady* points out, these bents are not all physical. Speech is important, because it reveals social class and education. So is dress. "Wear your dark blue jacket to the interview, not that ridiculous green one," the mother warns her son. Years later, now successful, he scans the clothes of the young job applicant in front of him with his mother's sharp eye!

Transferences are not all taught by words. Some just happen to impressionable children as they grow up. A son delights in his mother's perfume. Years later he detects it again on a woman he meets at a cocktail party. He likes her right away and doesn't realize why.

These subtleties powerfully influence us in our relationships with superiors at work. The most obvious transference is the expectation that our boss knows what he or she is doing and has the authority and influence to effect his or her wishes. Often it is not so much a rational belief in his or her competence and power as it is the child's feeling that the parent is omniscient, that mother and father possess complete or infinite knowledge, awareness, understanding, and control. This is an irrational omniscient transference that most of us feel. We may expect a boss's infinite knowledge, awareness, and authority to provide perfect care for us.

Our personal preconceived notions operate constantly and automatically. This is not all bad. It is, after all, what makes us avoid the shifty-looking person on a dark street at night as a potential mugger. Transferences need to be brought to consciousness only when they are causing repeated trouble. If we respond to every direction by a boss as though it were from some hated, controlling parent or dictatorial older sibling, it is essential that we understand the source of our irrational response and overcome it. Is this farfetched? Think of the people you know to whom you can't tell anything, let alone what to do.

Transferences can be subtle; they can erode our relationships with our superiors in a gradual way, without being noticed. Little things become big. "I can't stand his speech/his smile/ her smugness/his indecisiveness/his dandy dress/her flattery." Transferences can attract us to take jobs with superiors whom we later grow to hate. Transferences can close the mind to the real. They can distract us from our paths and make us feel that

advancement is hopeless when in fact it is not. Do not miscon-
strue all the strong feelings you have toward your superior as
based on pure fact. There is a lot of noise in the system—psychological noise.

Power

By definition, your boss can control and command you. Try to
think about his or her style and your response to it and consider
whether your transference makes you intolerant. It would be
wonderful if your chief were perfect, secure in exercising authority, fair and considerate, and open in accepting disagreement. But, like most of our parents, teachers, spouses, and
friends, your boss is likely to have one or more major weaknesses in the way he or she commands.

The greatest failing of an executive's leadership is not recognizing the proper time and occasion for the exercise of authority. He may be bossy about petty matters and fail to give useful
help about what really counts. She may suffocate her staff without adequately guiding it. Not giving you the direction you do
need, she persists in ordering you about when you don't require
it. Your boss may not formulate in his own mind what it is he
wants from you and yet feel dissatisfied that you haven't guessed
it. If he stopped and thought about it, he might realize that he
had put you in an impossible bind by resenting your questions
as evidence that you are too dependent or your lack of seeking
his advice as proof of your insubordination.

Not being directed properly can be very unsettling for any
employee, but more so for one with hang-ups from the past, one
whose parents were nondirective or too bossy, who is exces-

sively looking for help or rebelling against the arbitrary exercise of irrational authority.

It was necessary for John and another assistant vice-president to work together in order to automate their department, but they were squabbling and unable to move forward. John decided to go to Tim, their boss, for help, and Tim agreed on several different occasions to call a meeting to work out their differences so that the project could be completed. The job had been paralyzed for months, and still Tim did not move it ahead. John's patience was at an end, yet he saw no benefit to him from a confrontation with Tim over his failure to exert his authority. He decided to quietly document his efforts in several unsent memoranda, as insurance against the day when Tim's boss denounced Tim, who would then be likely to try to shift the blame to John.

John's initial response to Tim's frustrating behavior had not been so measured. Unconsciously reminded of his own father's passivity and lack of leadership at work and at home, John first wanted to go to Tim's boss and denounce him. It was only after he realized that it was his deep disappointment with his father that fueled his desire for a confrontation and that it would almost certainly be self-destructive (since the higher-up would side with Tim and criticize John) that he decided to be quiet.

A boss's reluctance to use his power can be almost as upsetting as poor timing and selectivity in using it. The nasty, unapproachable manager who lacks not only interest but the patience to listen can defeat all but the most secure employee. He or she may arbitrarily attack you rather than some specific part of your behavior. The overbearing superior may lecture you but fail to listen to your requests. An adequate exchange of information becomes impossible unless you break in on his or her closed mind. This is a hard situation for any employee, but especially so for one who has been cowered by a dictatorial parent and has no experience in making himself or herself heard. Many bosses are afraid of feelings. They hesitate to correct you or give criticism for fear of making you angry or upset. As a result, they are irritated with you but give you no hint of how to improve, or they may blurt out a sweeping denunciation that is totally unexpected and unhelpful.

Your boss may misuse his or her power over you for a variety of reasons. Making you jump may make her feel important. Insecure and possibly inferior, she may feel threatened by your greater talents. Salieri not only did not help Mozart, he sabotaged him. Your manager may play with you, keeping you dangling and upset. He may use you with no appreciation or thought of reward. Jealous of your talents, discomfited by your ambition, he may exercise his power over you to the point of cruelty.

Ben, a thirty-five-year-old middle manager ambitious to advance himself, had with his superior's full knowledge and support arranged a conference to which he invited several dozen potential corporate customers. Because of the excellent program he was able to put together, plus his savvy in promoting the event, it was well attended and resulted in some major orders for their division. The result in dollars exceeded Ben's wildest dreams, and he expected his boss to be not just pleased but excited. Instead, his superior acted oddly. He barely said anything to Ben, and took all the credit for his success. Ben was furious. His parents had always been quick to credit anything he did. His realization that it was unreasonable to expect his superior to be as generous as his parents helped him calm down. This didn't make him like his manager's hogging the credit, but it enabled him to accept it as an unpleasant reality and to begin to calculate how he could discreetly spread the word of his own contribution the next time.

What does a superior's incompetence, unpleasant style, or misuse of power have to do with transference? Everything! It is the experience you bring to your relationship with him or her that may cause you to respond in a self-defeating way. Transference may also make you unable to work with a boss whom the average employee would find acceptable. Look about you. Not every employee has trouble with a particular manager, or he or she would have been fired long ago. Of course, there are poor directors about whom almost everyone in the office would agree, but usually the trouble is personal and specific, influenced by one's own upbringing and expectations. The ways in which important family members handled your emotions when you were a child shape the way you manage yourself with your superior, especially when you believe him or her to be harsh and arbitrary in exercising power over you.

Most managers are not incompetent, dictatorial, abusive, or nasty. Their use of authority is comfortable and predictable. Nonetheless, the same manager may evoke trust in one worker, suspicion in a second, and anger in a third. This disagreement is based on the personal prejudices of transference. Your response is due as much to the result of your past experiences as of your objective view of your superior's behavior. One individual who believes the boss to be all-powerful might trust him to give a fair raise, while another might see him as withholding, interested in keeping down his overhead, and unlikely to give anything. The trusting worker waits securely for his or her just reward, while the doubting one experiences anger at expecting to be hurt.

Anger

You are probably angry at your boss for one or all of the following reasons. You asked her for the Friday after Thanksgiving off and she said no. She made you stay late the night you had basketball tickets. She barges into your office without knocking, interrupts your phone conversations, opens or reads your mail, bans you from key meetings, won't let you talk to important clients or customers, and ignores your best suggestions. The list could go on. These are not transference; they are real frustrations. What is a displacement from experience with parents or other important figures in your childhood is how you react to these actual wrongs. Transference affects judgments about whether you believe your superior hates you and wants to destroy you, is jealous of your good looks, intelligence, friendship with her supervisor, success with the opposite sex, social connections, or family money. And transference strongly influences how you respond to these real and imagined perceptions.

Bob had just turned thirty. Behind him was a career change, business school, and an unhappy year afterward in what he considered excessively harsh working conditions. Now he was in a new job. His present boss grew up on an Ohio farm. Bob considered his chief's schooling and work experience inferior to his own. He found his superior to be petty, controlling, and not only unhelpful but quick to block Bob's efforts. Bob had to find a way to work with this person whom he considered beneath him in education and ability, but he was so indignant at the man's stupidity that he was on the verge of leaving his job. My questions helped Bob to realize his intolerance for anyone he found less intelligent and to trace this back to his disappointment in his father. In fact, it was his mother's dissatisfaction with her husband that was at the root of Bob's problem. As a child, he felt powerless to help his mother, who complained continuously about her spouse's lack of material success, and he was upset with his father for not stopping her grumbling. When he thought about it as an adult, he remembered many happy moments with his father and realized that it was his mother's bitterness toward her husband that had poisoned his memory. Understanding this calmed Bob down enough that he was able to make a rational assessment about whether he could continue with his manager. He decided he would do better elsewhere and found a job working for someone he respected a lot more. Understanding the mental link between his boss and his father did not eliminate Bob's annoyance, but it did calm him so that he could act rationally. Without such understanding, the frustrations and irritations felt toward supervisors can bring back old deprivations, jealousies, and rages of childhood. Bob was angry at his manager not only because he reminded him of his father's ineffectiveness but for objective reasons, such as that he was petty, controlling, and blocked his daily efforts.

Employees want their ideas listened to, supported and tried out. When the superior doesn't do so, the underling feels mistreated and becomes upset. Often that frustration in the present kindles the same feelings that it did in the past, and the reaction is similar. If close family members handled anger by shouting at each other, the employee is tempted to do the same. But if past experience illustrated how to handle annoyances with a joke or to skillfully go around obstacles, instead of using energy to restrain a shout, the worker plots a thoughtful action to get his or her way, while covering any maneuvers with humor.

Since angry feelings toward one's manager are inevitable and can be a daily occurrence, it is not as essential that one understand why one is angry ("it is really toward my father";

"my father is great but my boss is a petty tyrant/treats me like a child/gives me no support/always criticizes/is too demanding") as it is that the reaction be regulated and hostile expressions carefully timed. As Aristotle wrote: "Anyone can become angry—that is easy. But to be angry with the right person, to the right degree, at the right time, for the right purpose, and in the right way—that is not easy." Most people stifle their irritation at work. Few feel free to vent their spleen at their boss—expressing hostility to your superior can not only prevent advancement, it can result in a pink slip. Shouting at those above you will not provide catharsis and relief but will produce anxiety and serious consequences.

The most common causes of anger are injustice, insult, and condescension. When the boss treats you unfairly, attacks your self-esteem, or behaves in an unpleasantly patronizing manner, you are likely to feel angry. Not only is it wise to control your rage, it is best to learn techniques of anger reduction so that your hostility does not seep out around the edges and poison your relationship to your superior. Here are some ways to calm your fury.

1. **Convince yourself that self-control is good for you.** The pendulum has swung away from the belief that catharsis and letting emotions hang out to be expressed freely are good for you. People do not get ulcers and high blood pressure from failing to shout at their bosses. In fact, it is just the opposite. The retaliation of your superior following your attack can hurt you much more than keeping your fury to yourself.

2. **Convince yourself that you can control your anger.** The way a person thinks about emotions influences behavior much more than most of us realize. "I couldn't help it—I lost

my temper" is an attempt to shirk responsibility for an action one later regrets. The idea of losing control is always associated with some negative event that is later disowned. No one ever says "I lost control of my kind feelings and helped a blind man cross the street." If you think of yourself as a hothead or someone who will take criticism from no one, change your attitude. You don't have to be a doormat or a silent masochist waiting to be misused, but you can be a person in control who expresses anger at the right time and in the best manner.

3. **Value the relationship over your emotion.** If you want to get ahead, you need your superior's goodwill. He must believe that you are for him, that you make his life easier, add to his reputation, and improve his profit record. Venting your rage because he didn't listen to a very good suggestion you urged on him will hurt your chance for more money and might endanger your job all together. Even though you've convinced yourself that you will be able to control your fury and that you won't get an ulcer by doing so, there are other things you can do to calm down.

4. **Rely on manners.** Manners are back in. For a while they were out, informality reigned, and etiquette was derided as artificial and stuffy. But observing the proprieties is an excellent way to manage anger. Say good morning to your boss, ask about her weekend and about the health of her family, even though she ignored your best suggestion and you remain furious. It's a good way to maintain cordial relations.

5. **Don't talk about it.** Telling your best friend or your family about how irritated you are at your supervisor not only does not let off steam, it may enrage you further as you go over the details, rather than trying to get over and forget them. The sympathy of your friend may increase your sense of injustice

and give you the courage to tell off the boss. It certainly is not wise to speak to anyone at work about your anger, since it may not only fan the flame but also might get back to the boss.

6. **Stay away.** This method is best used only for a short time, while your anger is hottest and you need to cool down. Too much avoidance damages your relationship with your superior. Workers who don't chat easily with their bosses don't get raises, and neither do those who are not available to help. So take a day or two to calm down, and then stop avoiding your superior.

7. **Use humor.** A joke eases tension. It is hard to laugh and hate at the same time. Try to kid yourself a little, perhaps about what annoyed you most. You could remark to your superior, in reference to that new project you've been pushing for, that you promise to stop referring to the present method as prehistoric. Don't make your attempts at joking too frequent or heavy-handed, and guard against cute digs under the pretense of fun, but if you can smile about your disappointment over his failure to take your suggestion, both of you will feel better.

8. **Act out a little.** This technique is tricky, but may help let off a little steam when used carefully. In general, it is best to remember that you don't have to let your anger out at all, but sometimes a little bickering or verbal dueling on some other matter than the actual one about which you are annoyed can ease the tension.

9. **Use your unique technique.** If you are one of the few who have reached adulthood, hold a full-time job, and don't have your favorite way to calm yourself when furious, then develop one in a hurry. Here is a shopping list of those that commonly work for others: strenuous (even violent) exercise, a long walk, a warm bath, a stiff drink (not too many), escapist fiction, music (soothes the savage beast), a movie, television, cleaning

the house, gardening, cooking, dancing, conversation with a friend. Some people pray, others meditate, and a few have developed very personal calming strategies, such as looking out a certain window at home or conjuring up a soothing memory. I have always been a little skeptical about the individual who says that when he is ready to kill his boss for exercising vicious power trips over him, all he has to do is think of the flower-filled field he played in as a child and tranquility rapidly returns. This always reminds me of Hollywood film sentimentality at its most syrupy, and I similarly do not believe the advice of behavior therapists who recommend that you summon this flowery field of childhood to mind as you are about to punch your superior in the nose. It is much better to convince yourself that being in control at such rage-filled moments is essential and that you are responsible enough not to lose it. Furthermore, you'll be damned if you will give the bastard the satisfaction of knowing his power trip has upset you that much. It is better to get even than mad, and it's wise to wait your turn.

10. **Useful retaliation.** There are ways to take your turn, to get back at the arbitrary boss who maliciously makes you jump through hoops. The trick is to wait until your action will effectively make her feel your sting and to do so in such a way that she cannot retaliate and hurt you further. It is difficult to advise what kind of retaliation you might skillfully apply, since each situation is unique. One strategy is to go around her and arrange a promotion within the organization but away from her. Another is to leave for a better job and at a time when she will feel your departure. Angry confrontations with your superior can never help you. To get back at her you have to be patient and subtle.

11. **Think differently about the annoyance.** Your boss asks you to go to Detroit to soothe a client. You regard this trip

as unnecessary and view the demand as further evidence of your superior's ineptitude. If you could think about the request in a different way you would not be annoyed. You might even see the Detroit meeting as a chance to demonstrate your skill in handling a disgruntled client.

If you try to empathize with your boss, you may find justification for his behavior that will soften your anger. A request that previously made you furious because you believed you were being insulted might now be viewed by you as evidence of your superior's insecurity. Although still annoying, it would be much less so. Our angry feelings are by and large morally based and arise when we believe we have been the target of an injustice. If you can see the boss's order that you go to Detroit as evidence that he is nervous about a client and not that he enjoys making you jump, you will be much less angry. If you are a little less self-centered in your irritation when he insists that you travel extensively to increase flagging sales, and realize that he is under severe pressure from his boss, you will feel less provoked.

The idea that you have about another's behavior sharply influences whether your reaction is angry. It can be valuable for you to think again regarding your snap judgment about why your superior ordered you to do a certain thing. You may find that he had a good reason or at least one that, even if you don't agree with it, was motivated by his own insecurities rather than a specific wish to humiliate you.

12. **Learn new and gentler reactions.** "No one pushes me around." "Everyone gets pushed around once in a while." "No one insults me." "All employees have to take a certain amount of criticism from the boss." "If he asks me to get him coffee once more, I'll tell him to go to hell." "I'm paid for my time and he can ask for anything he wants, providing it is legal

and moral.'' Thoughts can damage, and so can actions. It is wise to try to calm your temper, especially if you regard yourself as a hothead who has trouble getting along in an organization. Far from breaking your spirit, your new restraint will make you more cunning and capable. *Power over yourself will lead to power over others.* Slow to anger, you will enjoy self-control, uttering a gentle joke instead of an angry cry, polite chitchat rather than angry barbs. You will gain the ability to understand your superior's problems, not just your own. Rage can ruin your career. Cool control will make it soar.

Overcome Your Narcissism and Pay Attention to Your Boss's Needs

Every human being needs to be appreciated and cared for in some way. A sensible employee reminds herself every day that this emotional requirement is also present in the boss. It is worthwhile to stop and think about how you and your superior provide these essentials for each other. It's a two-way street, but most of us are much more aware of what the higher-up is or is not doing for us—being supportive, loyal, or helpful—and pay little attention to what we do for him. This variant of John F. Kennedy's dictum—ask not what your boss can do for you; ask what you can do for your boss—is the kind of attitude much more likely to lead to a promotion or raise. Of course, if your manager has very little interest in your welfare, it may make sense to find one who does.

Most of us do not want to be too dependent and demanding but can have a lot of trouble in specific instances, wondering what is reasonable and what is childish. Is it best to assume that mature adults live in a completely self-sufficient world, each like the lone cowboy on the frontier, relying on no one, or should we expect guidance from those above us in the organization? Are they to be regarded as coldly indifferent except when we make a mistake, when they chastise or fire us, or do we have a right to take for granted reinforcement, compliments, and encouragement? Are we adult if we expect lack of concern and childish if we anticipate praise?

In general, with both senior executives and their employees, the more focused a subordinate is on satisfying the needs of the boss, the more appreciated the subordinate will be. Nonetheless, some bosses are more caring and supportive than others. If you are having trouble deciding where your superior fits on the spectrum of cool to warm, there are several ways to think about the problem. Discreetly ask a few trusted friends in the organization how they perceive the boss. If they find her acceptable and you don't, the problem may lie in your being too needy. Was there a pattern in your dealings with past supervisors? Did you usually feel angry and unappreciated? If so, the fault is in you and not in the stars. But if on calm reflection, especially if a trusted friend or colleague concurs, you find your boss truly indifferent and uncaring, don't interpret your feeling upset as childish. Instead, take it as fair warning that you'll have a lot of trouble getting a promotion.

What Kind of Psychological Figure Is Your Boss to You?

Oh wad some power the giftie gie us
To see oursels as others see us!
—Robert Burns, "To a Louse"

Your boss may psychologically represent a sustaining, a supportive, or an equalized figure in your emotional life. The best example of a *sustaining figure* is a mother in her relationship to her infant; such a figure is perceived as one whom you cannot do without. If you are convinced deep down that you do not have the training or credentials for your job, that it is a fluke that you have it, and that only the tolerance, whim, or inertia of your leader allows you to remain, you believe that you derive your strength from your boss and that he is a sustaining figure to you. If most of the time you feel enraged toward your chief because you are convinced that he could make everything at work comfortable for you if he only lifted a finger, you have the attitude of an infant toward a mother who has the total power to make all well in the world. Very few people who are psychologically so infantile recognize it in themselves. Instead, they are convinced that the boss is no good. They cannot see themselves as others see them. Few of us are so completely immature, but many of us do have some infantile attitudes. The next time you are furious that an executive asked you to stay late to do an urgent task, try to calm yourself and see her point of view. Your mother wouldn't have been so tough, but the boss has a right to be.

The *supportive figure* is one relied on for aid and encouragement, but not, like the sustaining one, for absolute security. Rather than the infant, the analogy is to the child, who looks to the parent for direction and encouragement. The young child may accept being led more easily than the teenager who rebels. Again, the emotional reaction in the employee may obscure recognition of this type of immature reliance. "He never helps me do my job." "He never lets me think for myself." The feeling that the head person does not care or intrudes too much can mask the realization that an employee is like an adolescent. If you suspect you might need too much support, think about your past dealings with overseers. Have you often been angry at not getting enough help or at being controlled and directed too much? Is the fault in them or in you? If you keep encountering the same authority problem, chances are you have some growing up to do and need to become more comfortable with independence and dependence. Mature individuals accept responsibility and yet are willing to ask for help when they need it.

The *equal relationship* lacks the faults previously described but is not completely smooth and ideal. We all want the help we don't get and reject that which we don't need. Confusion and tension always cloud our judgments about our bosses. The mature worker at times must fight strong feelings of anger, dependence, and rebellion. He or she must agonize over whether to speak up or remain silent. But in an equal relationship, deep down the boss is regarded as a colleague with whom one collaborates to complete the task. If the grown-up employee assesses the head person as incompetent, unhelpful, or consistently obstructive, he or she may decide objectively whether it is wise to stay or leave. The decision is made coolly and rationally, using enlightened self-interest. In an equal relationship, it is not that boss and employee rank on the same level in the organization, but that they are psychological equals in the underling's mind.

There is a Chinese proverb that describes two fools as more intelligent than the greatest wise man. It is the sharing of ideas and suggestions between manager and assistant that yields a result greater than either could achieve alone. And it is in this spirit that the employee can approach the leader for a raise much more successfully than he could someone on whom he feels completely or even partially dependent.

What Kind of Psychological Figure Are You to the Boss?

Just as your feelings toward your boss are influenced by both psychology and reality, so are his toward you. He may imagine you are a "spoiled rich kid" when in fact you desperately need a raise. Or because you did not go to prep school, as he did, he may not consider you suitable for top management. His attitude toward you may not be influenced by social class, education, or money, but by your sex. He may have a stereotyped view of you as a woman and thus believe you are too dependent and emotional to be promotable. He may think you capable, devoted, and an expert at typing, filing, and the accounting system, but not slated for increased responsibility. Oddly, he may regard you as too good in your job and therefore indispensable.

Think about how he perceives you. This is a hard problem to solve, because few superiors will come right out and tell the truth, even at the annual review. But if a boss has never promoted a woman, or a prep school graduate, or someone whose skill he considered indispensable, chances are he won't advance you either, if you fall into one of these categories. How to attempt to change his view of you will be considered in detail in the last section of this chapter, but in general begin by first deciding if it is possible. If he never has given a decent raise to a woman and you decide he never will, go elsewhere.

Are the Boss and You Psychologically Attached?

In a rational world, employees would leave bad jobs and stay on at good ones. In reality, many workers remain long after they should have departed. Laziness? Yes. Afraid of change? Yes. But too often it is due to unrecognized attachment. John Bowlby, an English psychoanalyst, conceived of attachment as the "propensity of human beings to make strong affectional bonds to particular others" and to suffer "many forms of emotional distress and personality disturbance, including anxiety, anger, depression and emotional detachment" when separation and loss occur. This theory explains the strong ties between employer and employee that exist even when the relationship is poor. Thus, it can be almost as upsetting to leave a bad job as a good one. Even physical departure does not always break the emotional bond; witness the four firings of manager Billy Martin by New York Yankees owner George Steinbrenner. What makes Steinbrenner hire him over and over? It is because he admires his bad boy manager deeply and begins to miss him during the long season. And what causes Martin to be willing to work for this moody despot again and again? It is their deep emotional attachment to each other, one that includes intense love and hate.

An obvious and typical attachment is the one between the

vice-president for finances and Laura, his secretary for twenty-three years. She does everything, from the most menial task to protecting him against too many requests to calming his wife when she is upset with him. When he changed jobs, requiring a thousand-mile move seven years ago, she relocated with him. What does he do for her? He makes her feel that her work is important and she is indispensable. Laura does not work for money. Her boss takes care of her, and she feels rich enough.

A doctor and his office nurse, Beth, have the same attachment, but their relationship is not nearly so warm. He resents her compulsivity, her meticulous procedures and rules that needlessly complicate his work life. Beth's bossy and petty behavior annoys many patients, and he suspects that they may have lost more than a few because of her. The doctor not only never gives Beth a raise, he has thought of firing her. But then he sighs with resignation. He tolerates her and feels stuck with her for life. Being comforted by the presence of a familiar important person does not mean liking that individual or even being truly dependent on him or her. The doctor neither likes Beth nor needs her. In fact, he would be better off without her. But their hatred, as Elvin Semrad, the great Boston teacher of psychiatrists, observed, holds them stuck together like glue.

People at work become like members of one's family. Leaving them can be an emotionally wrenching experience. The effect of this attachment can strongly influence our careers and prevent us from leaving for a job with higher pay. Fear of being fired may stop an employee from aggressively seeking a raise. Because the breaking of an affectional bond causes anxiety and/or depression, many workers suffer with low salaries almost gladly in order to avoid the discomfort of thinking about changing jobs. The strong need to belong can undermine the confidence required to vigorously negotiate a significant pay raise. If important figures in the organization realize that you are tightly attached, they will have little incentive to give you more, because they already are sure they have you.

Making Others Perceive You as a Professional

Once you have overcome your most glaring immaturities and withstood the danger of the possible loss of your corporate family, you must present the new you to others. Your loser image, which kept you down, must be changed. This is no easy matter. But once you have truly convinced yourself, here is what to do to persuade those around you.

1. **Give your opinions in a brief and definite way.** A million qualifiers as you try to cover every possibility only bore those listening to you and make your stand seem wishy-washy and confused. Your boss is not interested in academic completeness but in a clear statement of what you think should be done and why. Give your reasons, of course, but keep it short.

2. **Take initiatives with customers and suppliers.** If you act like a leader, chances are your superiors will think of you as one. Thus, they will be inclined to promote you and to pay you more.

3. **Look for shortcuts and cost-cutting actions.** You will be thought of not as an assistant but as a person who saves the company time and money. Put your thoughts into action and present those above you with results, not a lot of smart talk. Contemplation doesn't yield success; doing something does.

When you ask for a promotion, it is very effective to be able to point to how much you have increased the profits of your department.

4. **Don't race out at five o'clock.** If you keep the hours of an underling and are viewed as a clock watcher rather than someone anxious to do a superior job no matter how long it takes, chances are you won't be rewarded. Show the executives you are as serious and hardworking as they are, and chances are you'll end up one of them.

5. **Dress like an executive instead of an assistant.** This helps your boss regard you as one of us instead of one of them. If your clothes show that your taste agrees with that of those to whose level you wish to be promoted, they will help you get there. Don't overdo and appear too rich and fancy, or you'll frighten off your superiors. Make sure you understand the dress style of those above you. If they are casually elegant, don't be formal. If they are conservative, don't be too radical.

6. **Be prompt.** Be on time to meetings, to work, everywhere. Show that you use your time well and that you respect others by your promptness. A good manager is efficient, not breathless and late. This is a good way to show that you are in control of yourself and the situation.

7. **Insist on respect.** If those on the next levels to which you aspire are addressed by their surnames, then insist that yours be used as well. It may feel funny at first, but remember that you are intent on changing your image. The discomfort you feel at first will soon give way to pleasure in your new status.

8. **Volunteer.** Take on new tasks not ordinarily associated with your present job. Make sure these are responsible and executive-like rather than menial and unpleasant. You are not trying to impress with how good you are at suffering, but with the fact

that you are management material. Don't confuse gratitude from the boss because of your willingness to do dirty work with his beginning to regard you as someone who is responsible and has contacts in the business community. Expand your responsibilities gradually so you don't upset your boss.

9. **Persuade your subordinates to take on some of your less desirable duties.** In return for helping a newcomer, try to get that person to do some of your petty chores. Not only will this give you practice in being an executive and motivating a subordinate to work for you; it will also free you to try more challenging tasks. Attempt to make contacts in the community that will be useful in your job. "I'll get those tickets for the client," you volunteer, thus impressing your boss. Don't tell her exactly how you found them, and make sure that you keep control of your sources. Knowing who might be interested in placing a larger order for your company's product or where you might be able to buy some raw materials more cheaply can make you a very valuable employee, one who will be given raises and promotions.

10. **Be patient.** This may be the last thing you want to hear, but it takes time to build your professional image. Don't expect to blind the boss with your brilliance. Even more important than being called by your surname or wearing the correct clothes, it is your persistent effort to be of increasing value to your company that pays off. Look to gradualism rather than the grandstand play.

11. **Keep your personal problems to yourself.** Complaining about your inability to find a good lover or about how mean your spouse can be or how defiant your adolescent son is can bore everyone. So can tales of your hangover. To some extent an office is a family, and you can talk to one or two close friends,

but your boss doesn't want or need to hear about your personal problems all the time. It hurts your professional image.

12. **Get along.** The most common reason for being fired is failure to get along with those with whom you work. Getting along means being cheerful and not wearing a long face. It means being cooperative and helpful to those around you. Do not act put-upon when asked to do something. The assistant account manager who refuses to stay late to work on a presentation may be within her rights, but she is less likely to be promoted or get a raise than one who is willing to help and be friendly. In your effort to take on new responsibilities so you can win a promotion and a raise, don't be too pushy. If your boss says no to one of your new ideas, try not to irritate him by insisting.

13. **Help the boss.** Your best efforts should not threaten your superior, but make her job easier and enhance her prestige. Don't worry that she will steal the credit for your work. What you have done will get out, and you must also learn to advertise yourself subtly.

14. **Keep your temper.** Losing it makes those around you lose respect and take you less seriously. Your being out of control puts them in control of you. If something angers you, deal with the offending person quietly.

15. **Establish priorities.** Going home exhausted because you worked eight, ten, twelve, or even fourteen hours doesn't mean you are doing well unless you spent the time on the most important parts of your job. You may be proud of your new idea for reorganizing your department, but the aim of the company is to make sales to customers. Make this your goal, too. Keep it in mind and you will get the promotions and raises you seek. Almost more important, you will get a sense of satisfaction at having met your objectives.

Management will be delighted by this new, professional, hard-driving you. You, after all, are the person they chose and trained. Your success reflects well on them. Your boss will feel like a proud parent whose child is successful. Organizations need new leaders. Headhunters search for competent individuals, who are always in short supply. Your ability and growth signal how well your boss has brought you along. Both of you will be proud.

Assertiveness and Preparedness

Assertiveness can be viewed as self-esteem put into practice. It is all but impossible to present yourself in a definite and confident manner if you feel stupid and ineffectual. Surprisingly, however, it can be done. In fact, there are two main theories about how to change your feelings of inadequacy. One way is to raise your self-esteem by analyzing its origins and learning to stop putting yourself down. The second is to act as though you are sure of yourself even if you aren't, and after a while you will begin to feel it. The first school is the psychoanalytic—your harsh parents continue to criticize via your superego—and the second is the behavioral, which endeavors to teach assertiveness training. My view is that it is like diet and exercise in weight-loss programs—both are necessary.

Knowing when and how hard to assert yourself can actually strengthen your self-esteem at the very uncomfortable time when you seek a raise and a promotion, and feel unsure about how much the company values you. Perhaps it will prove to be not very much. The uncertainty can shake the confidence of the most secure person. Being skillful in assertion can steady the nerves.

Everyone has trouble with assertion, especially in a pluralistic country like America. Putting yourself forward boldly and insistently means one thing in retailing and something very different in banking. A used-car salesman can push in ways the lawyer should not. What is proper behavior if your superior is of Middle Eastern background could be a disaster if he is Japanese. People from the Middle East stand close to one another and talk loudly, while the Japanese are distant and soft-spoken. Perhaps if the whole United States population were trained in one standard of assertion the problem of our pluralistic society would be overcome as one certified psychologically based mode became accepted. No longer Asians and Middle Easterners, Sicilians and Yankees, we would have become trained in one standard.

The key, therefore, to assertiveness is *judgment*—of who you are and who your boss is. What is appropriate to one business, to a particular situation, to a certain relationship of subordinate to superior, is not appropriate to another. That is why this book began with chapters on how you feel about yourself and your boss. Only after your emotions are in perspective can you begin to be confident in your ability to make that tough decision about how hard to push for what you want.

While confident people find it easier to be assertive than insecure ones, there is no guarantee that having confidence results in being assertive. People can be very good in their jobs and yet present themselves in a halting fashion. Certain of their ability, they nonetheless act indecisive and unsure. They fail to speak in meetings or take on leadership. They shrink meekly into the corner. Other factors besides abilities influence how one acts. Not surprisingly, these are determined by one's upbringing. As a child, were you encouraged to express yourself directly and forcefully or were you inhibited? Much has been written about how women have been taught to defer, not to appear too bright, to withhold what they know. Some parents encourage expressiveness and others meekness; some foster competitiveness and others cooperation.

Arthur is a brilliant accountant whose knowledge of the intricacies of the tax structure is dazzling, but he works for a small, sleepy organization with few clients. After a dozen years he earns about the same as a beginner in a big firm, even though he has become a partner. Arthur needs more clients. While playing golf, he became friendly with a potential wealthy one. For months Arthur schemed about signing up his new acquaintance, and finally, in their third year as a foursome, he said to his rich companion over a drink that he would like to devote all of his time to doing his tax work. Naturally, his friend did not leap at the chance of becoming Arthur's only client. In fact, he probably wondered why Arthur had so much time on his hands to devote to him. The accountants the tycoon was used to seemed desperately rushed. I interviewed Arthur, who told how his parents always encouraged him to be polite and truthful. They looked down on many successful business people as pushy, rude, and aggressive. They liked their mannerly, reserved, careful thirty-five-year-old son, and he liked himself. He too felt superior to those who were forceful. But still he wanted this man for a client. I suggested that he try to find out a little more about what his golf partner's business consisted of and then make some useful suggestions. To my surprise, he already knew the answers and had some excellent ideas. Arthur was sure of his skill but had no concept of how to present himself. The next time he got together with his friend and the subject turned to business, he offered a couple of his ideas. The man had already put some of them into practice, but several others excited and intrigued him. Before too long, Arthur was on the payroll.

Arthur had a skill to sell, but because he didn't know how

to present himself, his nervousness made him feel unsure that he had the necessary ability. Although it could be said that self-esteem is to the product as assertiveness is to marketing, if you don't know how to merchandise, you may begin to believe that what you are selling is no good. Thus, the circle: self-esteem influences assertiveness, which affects self-esteem.

Timing

Being cool, clever, and political means that there are times when you will say yes to the boss even though the dictionary definition of assertiveness requires you to put yourself forward "boldly and insistently." On certain days it is better to humor your superior rather than stand up for yourself. The righteously indignant person who always reacts with "how dare you ask me to do that" is unlikely to win promotions and raises. On the other hand, a coward who never opposes a superior's request will not win respect.

Timing, therefore, requires an acute awareness of the effect on those to whom one is expressing assertive behavior. Confident posture, good eye contact, and enthusiasm are called for every day, but saying no and expressing your own opposing wants, opinions, and ideas must come only at the right moments. Assertiveness must be handled with sensitivity to your subordinates, equals, and superiors, not flashed about like a dangerous weapon. Why emphasize this point to most of you, who probably consider yourselves too timid and unlikely to ever oppose a superior even at the proper moment? The reason is to increase your chance of success once you get up your nerve. If you pick a moment when your boss is enraged, exhausted, about to be fired, or submerged in red ink, the response you get will be likely to frighten you back into meekness. Proper timing will vastly improve your chances for success, which in turn will encourage you to express yourself more forcefully.

Force

Power can be exerted with a glance or a shout, a handshake or a gun, in the open or behind the scenes. When, how, and how hard to assert yourself constitutes a vast subject for your reflection. If your preferred style is a whisper but your superior is deaf, you may have to shout. If you are naturally ebullient and your boss is painfully reserved, perhaps you should quiet down. Your manager may not be deaf or reserved, but you may still be uncertain about how to behave. Should you act as though you are angry in order to get the notice to which you feel entitled or tolerate a particular injustice in silence?

Assertiveness exists on a continuum somewhere between compliance and aggression, both of which create problems, compliance because it presumably leads to becoming a misused victim, unrecognized and underpaid, and aggression because it insults and alienates superiors, who then retaliate by not promoting you or by firing you. But this is oversimplified. Powerful executives may lavish benefits on malleable underlings who do not threaten them while aggressive soldiers or ball players win rich rewards from their superiors. But insofar as the right image in most business organizations is to be confident and assured rather than timid or nasty, assertiveness is preferable to the extremes.

The relationship between feeling and behavior is essential

to the force and timing of assertiveness. It is best when one acts calmly and thoughtfully, aware of consequences and one's affect on others, rather than angrily. In business, as in poker, it is wise to mask emotions. In fact, regarding business as a game is one way theorists encourage participants to discipline their feelings. Holding anger in and waiting until you have calmly considered a course of action will not give you a migraine, ulcers, or worse. In fact, just the opposite is likely to occur. Raging at your boss will not make you feel better; it will get you no raise or promotion but eventually perhaps a pink slip. Calming down and approaching your superior according to a thoughtful plan that works can indeed make you happier. If you feel angry at your supervisor because your rights have been violated and you have been dealt with unjustly, the wrong can best be corrected by calmly planning how to go to him or her. A hostile outburst must be saved as a calculated last resort rather than be blurted out.

Being assertive rather than meek can get you into conflicts, which may make those above you very angry. Self-control means picking your controversies so they will do you the greatest good. It must be remembered, however, that putting yourself forward in a definite manner will usually win respect and make you valued, rather than result in battles. People with problems in acting confidently have them either with authority figures specifically or with everyone. They cannot be strong and firm because of insecurity and childhood training or out of fear of retaliation. The waiter in the restaurant who brought you a burned hamburger cannot hurt you if you send it back, yet the submissive person will say nothing. Those whose sole fear is retaliation may be savage toward the waiter and all others who are not above them, while cowering to their supervisors.

To my knowledge, no one has ever made a survey specifying how many employees require assertiveness training and how many need to learn aggression reduction, but I suspect that organizations select the submissive and that the overly hostile either don't join in the first place or are fired. Thus the emphasis here on the problems of the overly meek. They must change the way they see and present themselves. Let "the force" be with them. They need more of it.

Indirect Assertiveness

Being assertive usually implies stating your position directly and emphatically rather than operating deviously behind the scenes. But this definition focuses too much on style and not enough on what is much more important—results. If your superior gives you a time-consuming menial task to do that will produce nothing for your career even if you complete it well and efficiently, you have two choices. You can say no, which perhaps you should if this is the only kind of assignment you are given, or you can say yes but give yourself too much time for the job so you can fit in other activities more pertinent to your career advance. By not striving for perfection in routine detailed work and saving your energy for more challenging tasks, you change your boss's view of you from underling to potential leader. On the face of it you seem compliant, but secretly you are being assertive.

To exercise passive resistance, the stock-in-trade of the bureaucrat, you will have to do something about your guilt. Chances are your mother taught you to be honest and straightforward and punished you for being sneaky. Some parents seem to spend most of their children's adolescence trying to catch them smoking pot or necking in the back seat of the car. Privacy, for such individuals, becomes associated with guilty secrets, often sexual. For such people, operating behind the scenes seems Machiavellian and wrong. It is not a sin to outmaneuver your boss to get what you want: a promotion and a raise. Putting yourself forward effectively is smart, and it is assertive in the best sense. Sometimes this works much better than being open and aboveboard in your opposition.

If you try devious methods to get out of being choked by routine and noncareer-enhancing tasks given to you by your boss, you must learn to overcome perfectionism as well as guilt. Your mother taught you to be pleasing and your father to do your best. These virtues, when applied to mundane tasks like filing and typing, will keep your superiors happy and the child in you proud. It goes against the grain to advance yourself in a secretive way, but it is one grown-up trick that works well for your career. Remember, you don't want to be a perfect clerk all your life; you want to get ahead and make more money.

Not only might you feel uneasy at first when opposing and outmaneuvering your superior, you may indeed attract his or her displeasure. This can make you doubly nervous. One way to calm yourself a bit is to remember that you are trying to get recognition not as a faithful follower but as someone on the rise. You want and need recognition because of your leadership and creativity, not because you are a perfectly pleasing drudge.

Help Your Boss Be Assertive

The feelings and attitudes we have toward superiors—our transference—make us either expect them to possess the positive attributes we lack or, oppositely, exaggerate their faults once we learn that they have a few. Remember that your boss also fits somewhere along the continuum of compliance, assertion, and aggressiveness. If your manager is at either of the extremes, you will have trouble positioning yourself for your raise. The submissive superior will be reluctant to criticize you, worried that you will cry, get angry, or attack back. This can be a great problem for you when you try to set the groundwork for your raise at your performance review, because the acquiescent employer will find it hard to inform you of the faults that prevent you from getting more money.

One of the best ways to get ahead is to tell your superior about your goals and objectives for your career and then to get him or her to describe what, if anything, is standing in your way. Most managers will be reluctant to give you negative feedback, but you need to overcome their reticence in order to meet any criticisms and thereby remove the obstacles to your advancement. The compliant superior is the most difficult to get to level with you, but he or she can be encouraged to do so if you seem calm and genuinely interested in discovering your weaknesses and correcting them. It may be useful to say that you promise not to take the criticisms too personally but will use them as guides to better performance, which is in everyone's interest.

Another problem with the compliant boss is getting him or her to fight for your raise in the company. Such a superior does not like to upset higher-ups and will avoid asking or will take no for an answer too readily. You may have to make your boss more uncomfortable about saying no to you than he or she feels about seeking your advancement from those above. If your need for your immediate superior to like and approve of you is very great, pushing hard in this way can be difficult.

The aggressive manager presents the opposite problem. Far from being reluctant to provide criticism, he or she offers too much. You have to overcome the temptation to cry, attack back, quit, or be defensive or apologetic. The urge to argue and become antagonistic can be very strong. Obviously, it is difficult to get a raise from someone with whom you are having a battle. One effective method of dealing with an aggressive boss is to try to figure out what, if anything, is behind the attack. Is your manager under pressure from those above or afraid of being fired? Is there a personality conflict between the two of you that is severe enough to make it unwise to continue to work together, or is there a particular correctable underlying problem between you? If sales are down, causing your boss to be upset, get out and improve them and chances are the attacks will cease.

When you are pounced on by an aggressive superior, try to keep your wits instead of becoming antagonistic. It is never in your interest to have a no-holds-barred fight in which you say things that you will later regret and that can permanently damage your relationship with your boss. Admit your error if you've made one, but otherwise hold your ground and be firm. Repeat your supervisor's main point to show you've heard it, and if you do not agree, present your side with confidence. If the two of you remain far apart, try to bring the discussion to a close either with the respectful acknowledgment that you don't agree or with an effort to bring you closer together by suggesting an action toward resolution. You might advise consulting someone or looking up an objective source to settle your dispute. One other way to soften the blows of an aggressive boss is to recognize that it is your superior's way and not your fault. Thicken your skin, if you can, by getting used to the attacks and learning not to be too hurt by them. Try to assess the effect of the nastiness on your chances for a raise. If it looks hopeless, find a new job.

Before you decide to leave and only after you've tried everything else, you can blast your boss, loud and clear. Rehearse carefully so you won't say anything you'll truly regret in the heat of the moment, and then let your superior have it. This taste of his own medicine may bring him to his senses.

Are You Assertive?

While many people are quite sure of where they fit on the spectrum of compliant–assertive–aggressive, a large number do not know. If they are unassertive, the downcast face, tentative gesture, stooped posture, halting step, averted glance, and shaky voice are so much a part of their demeanor that they are unaware of how they present themselves. At the other extreme, the aggressive may get into battles and be repeatedly fired, yet be unconscious of why it is happening. They do not seem to realize how pushy and belligerent they are, how they dominate and humiliate others with their combative style. It might be worth your while, therefore, to think about where you fit on the scale. Answer the following questions yes or no.

1. Do you avoid all disputes?
2. Do you fight excessively with your boss and co-workers?
3. Do you look people in the eye?
4. Does your voice shake in meetings?
5. Are you able to express your opinions succinctly and forcefully?
6. Are you able to disagree without losing your temper?
7. Can you say no to unreasonable requests?
8. Can you lead others?
9. Are you able to make decisions without excessive agonizing?
10. Do you withdraw and daydream in a tough meeting?
11. Can you tolerate an occasional mistake?
12. Do you promote yourself?
13. Have you been fired frequently?

14. Could you call on your last bosses for recommendations?
15. Can you tolerate less than perfect work?

A compliant person will answer yes to questions 1, 4, and 10 and no to the others. Assertive and aggressive people will say yes to eleven questions but will differ on questions 2 (no, yes), 13 (no, yes), 14 (yes, no), and 15 (yes, no).

Adapt to Your Company's Ambiance

Think about the fundamental values and attitudes of your business organization and what role you play in them. If a dynamic and youthful atmosphere prevails and you are wearing twenty-year-old suits or dresses fished out of the back of your closet, invest in some new clothes, quicken your step, lose some weight, and act enthusiastic. If you work in the trust department of a bank and strive to appear reliable and trustworthy, youthful eagerness is out of place. It may depend on what you have been hired for and your continuing assessment of whether the company still wants your original role. A stodgy corporation hired a beautiful, outgoing young woman as an assistant finance officer in the hope that she would help management talk to one another. She tried, but many found her intrusive and offensive. In more conservative clothes and with a softer voice, she began to do better. She realized, as all must, that an assertive act must be carefully tailored for the specific audience.

One's assessment of the audience must be influenced as much as possible by reality and not by false assumptions and transferences. It must be affected not by what the organization says it wants, but by what it is really after. Your boss may announce that he wishes you to be creative and innovative, because it sounds good, while what is really sought is a pliable company person and team player. Test your supervisor gently to see what is really wanted. Don't be so sure that your predictions are infallible. The meek are too fearful of adverse consequences, and the aggressive not mindful enough.

The Courage to Fail

When putting your ideas or suggestions boldly forward, remember that you have a right to express yourself and be treated with respect. Most often you will not be attacked for uttering your opinions or asking for information you will need to do your work. Remember that a refusal is not an insult. If you are pounced on by your manager because of something you assert, that is not your fault. Supervisors are people, too, and sometimes they are nasty for no obvious reasons.

There is risk in putting yourself forward. The boss's response may not be predictable. You might step on his or her toes inadvertently and get a hostile reaction. Or you might make a mistake. It is worth thinking about your feelings about errors, because unless you are willing to suffer them, you will be unable to take responsibility for your actions. To be an executive requires making decisions involving large sums of money and extensive use of company resources on the basis of too little information. No one knows how many cars to build next year or the amount of beer to put in bottles.

If you had tough parents and unforgiving teachers, you may be one of the many adults who are terrified of blunders. And you will therefore have great difficulty putting forth your ideas and carrying out your plans. Because of your fear of errors, you will find comfort in a hostile dependent attitude in which you blame your superior for what goes wrong rather than yourself. Without a willingness to take charge, risk being wrong, and accept criticism for mistakes, you will not advance and earn more money.

Risk and the danger of mistakes are close companions. Taking a chance means that you may win or lose. Those who fear errors hide from risks. If you avoid taking a gamble and shun responsibility, it is unlikely that you will assert yourself and get ahead. The odds of your getting anything but token cost-of-living salary increases are slim if you are unwilling to face uncertainty.

Stake Your Claim

From one point of view, titles don't mean much. You can be called director of research and development, but if you are too timid to act the part, your rank becomes meaningless. Perhaps it isn't your own reticence but your supervisor who blocks your way. One way that supervisors get submissive employees to do menial tasks is to give them fancy titles. A manager may be one on paper but not in reality. Let your boss know that you are someone to be reckoned with, that you are a strong person who expects to do what you agreed to when hired and not a lot of routine work. This means saying no directly and indirectly. It may even lead to confrontation and the need to leave your job. But in order to show that you are serious, you have to be willing to see the conflict through to a conclusion. This does not mean that you should be a prima donna, unwilling to do any unpleasant tasks at all, but it does require determination to stand your ground firmly. The ability to obtain what you are after without alienating others or infringing on their rights is the object of assertive behavior. Making the title you were given meaningful and converting your promised job description into reality may require toughness on your part.

Steady persistence is required to firm up a new position or advance an old one. Although flexibility and cooperation may require you to pitch in on clerical and other unpleasant chores from time to time, your unvarying expectation remains the same. You must be convinced that you are a leader in order to persuade others. When your superior asks someone else to perform an executive action that you believe to be one of your functions, don't be afraid to say "That's my job and I will take care of it." Stake your claim or it will be lost.

Final Preparations

Your self-esteem is high. You approve of the energy and skill with which you are performing the highest levels of your job, the aspects that make you most promotable. You are convinced that you are worth a raise and would give yourself one were you in your supervisor's position. You have worked on your relationship with your boss, ridding yourself of as many of the transference and neurotic aspects as possible. In fact, you have good feelings toward your superior, which so far as you can tell are returned.

You have been working on your manager to convince him or her of your worth, a public relations effort in which you casually recite your successes. "This quarter sales are up 22 percent." "We have sent out twice as much promotional mail as ever before and it's paying off.'' Your long day at the office extends from early in the morning to well after 5:00 P.M. Your energy, enthusiasm, and inventiveness have been apparent. You assert yourself in ways that are effective, not obnoxious. Your superior seems to be pleased with your work, and the company is thriving. Not that business is the best it ever was, but there have been no recent tragedies, big orders lost, or enormous deficits discovered. It seems to be a good time to try for a raise.

Timing, of course, is important. It is easiest when the general economy and your particular firm are thriving, but sometimes you have to go for it at a lean moment. Otherwise you might have to wait three years until things turn around. If your contributions are very strong, even if the company as a whole is not doing well they may not be able to afford to lose you. Don't be demoralized by management's talk of salary freezes or losing quarters. Without you, losses might be greater, and company policy can always be bent or stretched for an outstanding employee.

Before making an appointment to talk to your supervisor about salary, in addition to your campaign that presents you as assertive, energetic, and of great value to the company, you might drop hints that one or more competitors are interested in you. While you should not threaten to leave unless it is absolutely necessary, it can be useful to let your superior know directly or indirectly that a headhunter has called or a friend told you about a certain position that is available. One executive asked his superior if it would be all right to talk to a client of theirs who wanted to hire him, but most employees are not so open and choose to leak the information in a less direct way.

Do salary research. What are others with similar responsibilities making in your or other organizations? Ask friends, colleagues, and headhunters, and go on some job interviews to find out what you are worth. The recent history of wildly escalating baseball players' salaries is a striking example of how much money can be earned if an employer cannot take you for granted but must compete to keep you. If you know what you are worth and what is reasonable, you are in a much stronger position when you talk to your superior about salary. You will not feel or appear helpless, but will be intelligent and persuasive. You are not begging for a handout, but simply asking for what you are worth. You know how important you are to your boss, and simply expect the company to pay for it.

One further word about timing: pick a moment before salary decisions have been made rather than after. Your superior will be in a better frame of mind to consider the subject than if he or she had just reviewed everyone's salary and closed the subject for the next six months. Do not choose a Monday morning, when your supervisor is occupied with a pile of mail, or a Friday afternoon, as he or she is rushing off to spend the weekend out of town. Pick a midmorning time on a Tuesday, Wednesday, or Thursday, and call for a meeting. On the phone say openly why you have asked to get together with your superior. Say that you would like to discuss your future and your salary needs. Having set the time and place to culminate your campaign, start to rehearse.

The Rehearsal

It is 6:00 P.M. the evening before the meeting and your superior has gone home. Go into his room and practice talking to him. "Excuse me, but I've come to speak to you, as you know, about my salary. Would you mind if I shut the door?" You need the door closed for privacy and to prevent or at least minimize interruptions. Sit down in the very chair you will occupy the next day. Get right to your subject and do not speak of other matters. You are not in this closed office to discuss an order that must be filled. "I would like to talk to you about a raise," you begin. Go through your speech. Anticipate his replies as much as possible and try to counter any objections. In the last chapter I will go over some common ways bosses turn down raise requests and suggest ways to counter these. If you have any evidence of being underpaid, use it. Summarize your importance to your superior. Do not threaten your boss or get into an argument. Your object is to get a raise, not your superior. You do not want to do anything that will jeopardize the good relationship you have built over many months. Start gently and get tough later only if absolutely necessary.

Pay attention to your feelings as you begin your practice session. Of course you feel scared. It is normal to be worried about being turned down, but if your fear is excessive it will paralyze you and make you unable to plan what you will say. It is also abnormal for nervousness to become so strong that you become convinced you will fail no matter how hard you try. At that point anxiety ceases being a motivating force that helps you carefully plan your strategy for tomorrow's meeting and becomes counterproductive. If you feel certain your superior will never grant your request, you can become unwilling to ask for a raise at all, or you may do so in such a tentative fashion that you will too readily take no for an answer. This is a crucial matter. By being so afraid of your manager's negative response, you inadvertently end up saying no to yourself. Even if you force yourself to march in tomorrow, the way you ask can doom you. Your manner can betray you, and if your boss picks it up he will be able to tell that you don't really expect more money and that you are asking only as a matter of form. The excessive fear of being said no to can become a self-fulfilling prophecy.

Be very careful to understand that tomorrow's exercise is not a charade and that you indeed deserve a raise.

If excessive anxiety can trip you up, so can your feelings about money. High on some workers' lists are pride in the quality of performance, loyalty to the company, colleagues, and customers, and interest in solving challenging problems. Even when such people suffer from severe shortage of money, they seem curiously resistant to going after more dollars. They may be angry at not having been recognized and given significant sums but will not initiate tough salary talks. These nonmaterialists are proud of their lack of interest in the coin of the realm. Money to them is dirty and déclassé. In fact, they usually are masochists who unconsciously damage themselves. They explain their lack of means to live in a good house, travel, provide for their children, wear fine clothes, and drive a nice car as being caused by cruel bosses and ruthless competitors. They regard themselves as aloof from the money-grubbing marketplace or as victims of it, but they do not see their own self-damaging tendencies, their need to be poor. Their nonmaterialistic naïveté keeps them penniless and punished. They are ready to accept the boss's refusal to give them more money, and some even exercise their power over a superior in a perverse way by making sure of being turned down.

Pay attention to your feelings about money. Certainly there are many work pleasures other than the financial. Enjoying colleagues and customers, creating something, performing a service well, building a better product: all may give as much or greater satisfaction than carrying home cash. Your earnings, however, are a reward for what you do, a sign from your superiors that your efforts are appreciated. In most companies the raise is calculated on performance and the worth of the employee. A minimal raise can be a signal to look elsewhere for a job. While money may not be the most important aspect of your job to you, it nonetheless has a primary place. It can be useful and provide pleasure for you and your family.

Examine your attitude about money carefully to see if it is of the "either/or" variety—that one either has high ideals concerning one's career or is a money-grubber—and try to resolve your extremism so that you can keep your noble feelings and still support yourself and your family adequately. Having a right to a fine, nicely furnished home, interesting vacations, well-tailored clothes, and a decent automobile does not mean that your values are false and that you are hopelessly selfish. In fact, it may mean that emotionally you have taken the final step into maturity, from being a deprived child to being an affluent adult.

Having found that you are neither pathologically afraid nor scornful of money, you still find yourself uncomfortable. Even though you have been doing an excellent job and believe your performance warrants a significantly higher salary, you still feel uncertain of yourself. This is normal. Self-esteem is variable, and whenever you face stresses it can go down. A woman received an unexpected letter from her new boyfriend. She panicked and thought, "He doesn't want to see me anymore." In fact, it was a warm note. A young physician was called in by the head of the medical unit. He worried that he was going to be reprimanded or fired. In fact, he was asked to participate in a research project. The dean addressing the newly admitted freshman class gets a big nervous laugh when he says, "Each of you thinks she got into this school by mistake."

If you are nervous because you don't think you deserve a raise, in spite of your hard work and serious effort, recognize your normal insecurity and conquer it so it will not defeat you tomorrow. Another way to overcome your shakiness is to get just a little angry. You are going in to get the raise you should have been given without asking. If your boss weren't preoccupied or, worse, indifferent, you wouldn't be going through this anxious preparation. The company is happy to take your long hours and inventive effort, but slow to reward. "Dammit, they owe me a raise!" Why should you be driving that rusted car or be unable to make home improvements, or to rent that new apartment on the river? What is important, a decent living standard for you or only slightly larger profits for some already rich stockholder? Anger helps drive away fear and insecurity. Of course, you don't want to attack your superior tomorrow, or you'll fail to get what you want. But a little righteous indignation gets you up for tomorrow's game.

Check your attitudes for passivity. The structure of many large companies with strictly established policies regarding advancement in job level and raises can foster a static feeling in employees, which in the most bureaucratic of settings is perhaps warranted. If your organization is so clearly defined that there is no way for you to get more than the 6 percent annual raise dictated by an enormous number of rules and fine print, perhaps this book is not for you except insofar as you are dissatisfied with having your future so precisely spelled out. After all, asking for a raise is an anxiety-provoking experience, and perhaps you so fear this that you work in a setting in which this is not necessary.

But if you are sick of being so defined or if your organization is more flexible, go ask. You may discover that although you thought your boss couldn't promote you faster than the rules allow, formulas are for the sluggish and the person of energy can get them bent. If your boss wants you, he'll find a way to advance you and give you raises to keep you motivated and happy. From his point of view, hungry workers are the best, and those content to operate within a real or imagined inflexible framework of promotions and raises are not worth as much.

It's a Game

Regarding it all as a game helps calm you so you can get emotional distance from what will happen tomorrow. While a rehearsal can provide effective mental preparation and strategy, you cannot anticipate everything, nor should you try to. Not only might there be surprise, but spontaneity is important and you don't want to be stale and overprepared.

And it is a game, after all. In most cases your boss is a professional manager, not the owner of the business. She will not be giving you a raise out of her pocket. The money she is using can be regarded as Monopoly money. It is a tiny fraction of a percent of the budget, although it may mean a decent apartment to you. What your superior may need is a reason to give you a raise, one that she can justify to her boss or to the finance committee. So your manager is not involved on the level of her pocketbook but may be afraid, like a parent, to give one of the children more money than the other because of jealousy. You cannot let this concern you too much. After all, they may also be underpaid and afraid to ask for more money. Take the attitude that you should have your due, and if they don't have the energy to go after theirs that is not your problem and certainly not a reason for your request to be denied.

As you sit in your boss's office, think of yourself as a player in tomorrow's game, psyching yourself, getting yourself up so you can win. The opponent, your superior, may not even be against you. You will read the other side tomorrow and respond to their game plan. Will you be given a sob story about the business? Will an attempt be made to buy you off with a title but no money? What kind of defense will be offered and how hard should you go at it?

One very effective way to enter a session asking for a raise is to get an offer from a competitor. Superiors often shape up when their employees are courted by others. It is human nature to take an old, faithful employee for granted. In fact, the best time to get a raise is when taking a new job. When they want you and don't have you is the best opportunity to get money out of employers. The competitive offer must be handled delicately or you will alienate both your present and future superiors. Many bosses will take the position "You can't threaten us" or "This firm is so fine that you should be thrilled to work here for less." Agree that you are indeed delighted to be associated with excellence, that you remain highly motivated and interested, but that you cannot continue on your present salary and wish your company would meet the other firm's offer.

So long as you realize that tomorrow's session is a game, you'll be able to go very hard at the boss without fearing an uncontrollable, angry response. After all, football players bang heads, but once the whistle blows the violence stops. Your superior has been asked for many raises before. It may be your first time, but it isn't his or hers. Your boss may have a buried sense of amused detachment, while observing how you ask for what you want. It is a ritual to him or her and, realizing this, you should try to impress with your performance to show your bargaining ability at its best.

Negotiating a Raise

The moment you have rehearsed for has arrived. You are well prepared and your emotions are in control. Having done your job very well, your self-esteem is high. You have discovered and discarded any childish attitudes toward your supervisors. Neither aggressive nor meek, you are set to assert yourself calmly and effectively.

Before you see your superior, it is essential that you have clearly in mind what your strengths and options are and how you want things left if you do not get what you want.

Strengths and Options

If in your industry forty-five-year-old vice-presidents like you are usually fired and replaced by twenty-six-year-old MBAs at half the salary, unless you possess some unique and irreplaceable talent, such as a special relationship with powerful clients or the ability to bring in far more business than some green youth, you are unlikely to get a raise. If you have determined that you have real strengths, measured in terms of your special value to the organization, consider your options. These consist of other available opportunities plus your real needs.

Most alternatives do not pursue you but have to be searched

for. The most effective way to discover options is to seek them out and have real offers in hand before going to your boss for a raise. If you earn $23,000 a year and have an attractive offer for $27,000, you know someone wants you and for how much before you begin your negotiation. Obviously this will put you in a very different frame of mind from fearing you will be out on the street, penniless, should you decide you can no longer work for the salary you now receive. And since you must have money to live, you know before negotiating that you will continue to work for the same wage should your request for a raise be refused. This lack of a better alternative may not stop you from going after more money, but it will influence you to take no for an answer if that is what you get. Should you be turned down, whether you have alternatives or not, you may decide to lessen the negative impact by saying "I understand that business is such that you cannot give me what I want now, but I intend to talk to you again in three months or as soon as business improves."

A Different Kind of Negotiation

Your employer wants you happy and highly motivated to do a good job. There is no victory when you leave disgruntled because you feel underpaid and unappreciated. Your employer does not win when you lose. If you pay too much for your new automobile, the salesperson gains a higher commission but is unlikely to see you again. While he or she would prefer that you be satisfied, in order to get more business from you and those you might influence, the main motivation is to make the most money. Your boss is more like your spouse. No one wins in marital disputes, and it is in the partners' interests that the two remain happy. Like the extreme measure of divorce, being fired or quitting terminates the relationship. While people work together it is in their mutual interest that both be happy.

The boss plays a role against you in salary negotiation but isn't really your opponent. He or she is ambivalent: *responsible* to upper management's desire to keep overhead down, yet *responsive* to you so that you will be happy and motivated. In most cases the money does not come from your superior's own pocket. What is important isn't who wins on the day you go for a raise, but that both parties go away victors. You are pleased with getting more money, and your manager feels happy at having a first-class worker. It is your job to persuade your boss that he or she wins when giving you a raise.

Your Feelings at the Moment of Negotiation and How to Overcome Them

No matter how unneurotic and mentally prepared you are to seek a raise, you will have strong emotional reactions at the time you actually do it. Partly this is because it is stressful to petition for more money. The strain comes both from having to ask and from anticipation of the answer. We would all prefer to be given exactly what we want or need without having to request it. Needless to say, this almost never happens. Having to ask is an emotional event for most people. An employee can become angry that his or her contributions were not recognized and rewarded. Feeling this anger can trigger defenses against expressing this uncomfortable emotion. Avoidance is one of these defenses. Afraid of exploding in rage, the individual decides not to ask at all. "My boss will have to come to me," is the reaction of some proud employees. Other employees experience the need to ask the boss for a raise as a form of begging and a loss of independence. Emotionally they feel like powerless children who are demeaned by asking for money. The more defeated worker assumes that the manager is the equivalent of a stingy parent who will refuse even a reasonable request. While there indeed are neurotic bosses who are miserly with money that belongs to the firm and would best be used to reward and encourage employees, in most cases it is the raise seeker's irrational fear that lies behind this dire prediction.

The best way to calm your feelings about having to negotiate for more money is to start by realizing that you won't get a raise without asking. Try to calm your anger at your superior with the knowledge that businesses do not give money away readily. Focus on your expectations regarding your employer's response when you make your request. Most likely it will not be one of outrage and criticism; rather you will be regarded as a serious professional concerned about your career path. Furthermore, remember that a raise is not a favor and it is not demeaning to ask for one. It is part of your manager's job to listen to your petition for more money. It is a sign of your commitment to your career and a demonstration of your ability to talk to higher-ups in a controlled way. Your boss has requested raises in his or her day and recognizes your attempt for what it is, one part of the institutionalized drama of work life. Your effort will be regarded with curiosity and perhaps even with admiration.

No matter how prepared you are, you are likely to have one or more of the following central, underlying feelings just before and during the negotiation. They are normal, situational anxieties and must be both tolerated and overcome.

1. **Defeat.** The night before, or perhaps even as you sit in your superior's office, you feel the silent certainty that you cannot win. Remember that anxiety at such a moment is normal and that part of normal stress is a sense of impending doom—in short, of failure. Being defeated before you begin is a way to avoid the uncertainty of trying and the aggression required. Defeatism is a common, normal feeling that must be overcome.

2. **Fear.** This emotion is accompanied by several common thoughts, some of which seem almost rational. In fact, they are not; they can stifle what would otherwise be a successful salary negotiation. Worry about taking risks, about losing a needed job when you have a family to support, about being one little person against a huge corporation, about losing a secure and familiar position, about not seeing your friends at work any longer, about being embarrassed by being told by your boss that you do not deserve the raise you seek—all these fears can seem more or less valid reasons not to try or to make a cursory effort while readily accepting your superior's polite refusal that a raise for you just isn't in the budget at the moment.

3. **Attachment.** There is security in familiar surroundings and people, and distress when one is separated from them. This is a human characteristic present in all of us from childhood to old age. Each of us possesses a basic human conservatism against changing our routines, and each of us wants our life history to proceed without interruption. What causes us to accept the discomfort of separation is the expectation of something better. As with most human emotions, some individuals experience them

more painfully than others, probably as a result of an inherent sensitivity of the nervous system as well as childhood experiences. Fear of loss of attachment may be very powerful and cloud the mind with such beliefs as "No other company would have me at this stage of my career." It is extremely unlikely that your skills are of no use elsewhere. You are suffering an irrational attachment, which can be overcome by looking around a little to see if there is any interest in you elsewhere.

4. **Sympathy.** Some workers avoid the fear and distress that normally accompany asking for a raise by indulging in almost maudlin sympathy for the boss, the company, or less advantaged employees. They don't want to put their superior through the stress of having to negotiate for a raise because they feel sorry for him or her. Or their loyalty to the company makes them unwilling to make it pay them more. Finally, there is the feeling that since they earn 10, 20, or 100 percent more than so and so, it is wrong for them to seek higher wages. In almost every case this sympathy is ill-founded and should be fought against in order to successfully negotiate a raise.

5. **Rage.** It is natural to be angry at your superior if you feel underpaid and therefore unappreciated. Why should he or she have a beautiful summer home, a superb apartment, and beautiful cars and clothes while you live modestly, painfully struggling to pay your bills? The more you see your superiors as withholding and the more you feel used and misused, the greater your rage will be. The degree of your anger is influenced not only by the realities but by how emotionally reactive you are. In the animal kingdom, rage leads to fight or flight, but neither of these would produce a successful outcome to your quest for more money. Your anger must be held in check so you can operate effectively to get what you want and deserve from your manager.

Mastering Your Feelings

The five feelings just described must be mastered in order to complete your negotiations for higher pay successfully. The first step is to distance yourself from the force of your emotions. Remind yourself that what you are experiencing is normal, common, and expectable. It is part of the salary-raise ritual, a game that you would play better if you were less excited. Focus on your future goals rather than on your past fears and angers.

Transform your feelings about negotiating for more money: change impediments into advantages. If angry, don't let yourself withdraw or attack your boss, but use your conviction that you have been wronged to motivate you to right the situation. If when reading the message from the pit of your stomach you discover that you feel defeated or fearful, calm yourself with the thought that the worst your boss can say is no and that then you will decide what to do about it. You may choose to accept it, satisfied that you have tried your best, or perhaps you will decide to find a new job. Whatever happens, you will undoubtedly feel better than if you had done nothing at all. Taking action enhances self-esteem, while failing to do so lowers it. Go ahead and try.

Feelings of attachment and sympathy are kind, and you should not be ashamed of loyal feelings, but you have to be on your own side in order to get ahead. Your boss—whom you may like and even feel sorry for because he or she has a lot of professional or personal problems—will not be hurt by your seeking more money. Your doing so is a professional act, not a personal one against him or her. In fact, you would be wise to believe that it is to the advantage of both you and your superior, as well as the company, to give you a raise. You are not acting against those you like so much as on behalf of yourself, as any professional would.

Take Stock of Your Strengths

Having faced and overcome your weaknesses, it is time to take stock of your strengths. That assessment will add to your sense of power and mastery as you enter salary negotiations. The most important thing to realize is that the boss needs you because you make him or her look good to those above and that you also satisfy his or her needs. In addition, it would require a lot of time and energy to replace you and train your successor. Therefore, it is definitely in your boss's interest to keep you and for you to be happy.

Not only does your boss need you, but he or she will regard you as more professional for seeking a raise. You will not lose your job if you take care not to damage your relationship with those from whom you want more money. A negotiation can be very hard-fought without hurting the feelings of those involved. In the heat of the moment do not threaten to leave if you don't get your way unless you have someplace better to go. But even if you do say you'll leave, you do not have to do so unless you have destroyed your relationship with your superiors. This will not happen even in the toughest negotiation if the focus is kept on the issues and not on the people.

You have the power to leave and work elsewhere, especially if you have done your research and found a desirable alternative or two. Bosses do not like it when you leave them. Your final advantage is your preparation for the meeting. Since you have controlled the timing of the discussion and prepared for the event over weeks or months, you have the advantage. Use it!

Effective Tactics in Negotiating a Raise

It is essential that you keep in mind your main goal, which is to show your boss that he or she wins when you get a raise and a promotion. Your superior's victory is a happy, cooperative, motivated, hardworking employee. In order to achieve your aim, you must be tough about what you want without being hard on your manager. The two of you will have to work together after this, so you do not want to damage your relationship. Firmly go after what you are convinced you deserve, but don't be obnoxious, threatening, or out of control. Remember, too, not to stray from the main point of the salary negotiation onto problems of the organization that are interesting and of mutual concern but not relevant to your goal. If you allow your focus to be shifted more than momentarily, your effort will fail.

Beginning Tactics

1. **State your goal immediately.** Do not hesitate or get into small talk. If your manager tries to change the subject, politely respond to the comment, but then quickly return to the main issue. Open the meeting with a line such as "I'd like to talk to you about a raise and a promotion." If the meeting is not one you have called for, but an annual or semiannual performance review, you might send a memo a day or two in advance summarizing your accomplishments since the last review, including new knowledge and skills you have acquired and your

plans for the future. This will help your manager, since he or she is not nearly so aware of your effectiveness as you are.

2. **Emphasize your accomplishments rather than your personal needs.** Your employer is interested in how you have increased sales or the efficiency of your department, not in whether you can afford designer clothes or a quality automobile. Recite your record succinctly and with conviction. If you don't seem proud of it, your boss won't be impressed either.

3. **Start each discussion on a point of agreement.** You and your manager are a team. What you do for yourself and the company is also something you have done for him or her. Comments such as "We've done very well in this department, and as you know sales are up 30 percent; I think my contribution in the marketing area has been substantial" and "I know we've had a tough year, but I'm sure that my contribution in the new-products division will make next year much more profitable" are remarks that influence your boss much more favorably than ones that suggest argument and strife.

Middle Tactics

4. **Name an initial salary 20 percent over what you expect.** It is best for you to name the figure you want first, so that you don't end up defensively arguing against a low one suggested by your superior and so that he or she doesn't become attached to such a dollar position. If the boss appears shocked by your request, remember not to let yourself feel too upset. It is a tactic much like the car salesperson's pain at what he or she considers your ridiculous offer. Answer your superior's ploy with a calm recitation of your value to the company, and remember that it is usually not your boss's money. You and your superior are taking part in a ritual, and the best way to win is to remain

calm, observe your opponent, be polite and good-humored, and stay firm.

5. **Pay attention to your own nonverbal behavior.** If your manager tells you that the company is having a bad year or that those with more experience don't earn the amount you request, watch that you do not nod your head. We all tend to make this unconscious social response. The next time you tell a story at a dinner party, pay attention to the nods and "uh-huhs" your words elicit. It is the polite way we normally reinforce one another to show that we are listening and that we agree. You do not want to unconsciously give the impression to your boss that you agree that there is no money for your raise or that it would be out of line compared with more experienced (and perhaps valuable) employees. Do not nod your head; instead, to show that you have heard, paraphrase your manager's words in the following manner: "I understand that you are under the gun to cut overhead for next year, but I think that my experience and the plan I have developed will diminish your overtime costs substantially." Remember, the way to make money is with skilled employees doing their jobs efficiently and well, not with poorly paid, substandard, and disgruntled ones. If you convince yourself that giving you a raise is good for the company, you will better be able to persuade your superior.

6. **Repetition.** Repeat your points using different language. This helps make sure that your superior hears them and also shows that you mean business. Repetition is a very effective means to emphasize your salary requirements.

7. **Silence.** Silence is an extremely effective tool in a negotiation. It gives both sides time to think, to evaluate both their own and the other's position. It also is uncomfortable and constitutes a pressure. Your lack of response may force your boss to speak. If he or she has just made you a salary offer and you

say nothing, your superior will feel that you have rejected the offer. In the best of circumstances, your manager will be pressured into making another and better one.

8. **Use eye contact.** We express a lot with our eyes: love, fear, and hate can all be reflected in our lingering look. In a staring contest, one person attempts to force another to lower his or her gaze. Naturally, you want eye contact to be friendly in this negotiation, expressing neither fearful avoidance nor hostility. You cannot do much about your superior's glance except to make yours receptive, but you should look at your listener without staring in a way that would make him or her uncomfortable.

9. **Say no when necessary.** If you cannot continue to work for the amount named, you will have to say no to a particular offer. Wait for a new offer, and if your superior will not negotiate further, name a figure yourself. If you have previously done so and the two of you remain far apart, either suggest a recess until the next day or begin to discuss how far apart you are and ask your superior to try to help you resolve the ·problem. Ask questions about why your boss feels he or she cannot increase your salary, and show you understand and are sympathetic to the concerns and difficulties. Do everything you can to keep this from becoming a stalemate and a contest of wills. Suggest an objective criterion, such as a newspaper ad for a job similar to yours at the salary you seek, or mention a job offer you have at a higher amount. This would be the moment to use salary arbitration if such a mechanism exists at your company.

Another way to overcome the impasse is to create other options if possible. You may elect to accept your present salary temporarily while business is bad, but announce that you will be back in three months to try again. If you do agree to postpone your raise, remember to actually make an appointment before the three-month deadline. Don't be angry that your boss didn't remember the date and call you in. One other option is to acknowledge that business is bad but to say that if your plan to improve profits works, you will expect your raise to be retroactive to the date of this negotiation. It would be wise to get such an agreement in writing, since your present superior may no longer be in the same position in three months or may forget the agreement.

10. **Try to make your boss an ally in your effort to get more money.** Fundamentally, it is not against your boss's interest to get you a raise and a promotion. Therefore, try not to treat your manager as an opponent but as a collaborator. You might say, "We work together and it is in both our interests that we be happy."

If your boss is opposed to your raise, make an effort to understand the reasons. Paraphrase his or her words: convince him or her that you have heard and understand. This technique prevents the executive from concentrating on getting his or her point across and puts him or her in a mood to listen to yours. Ask if there is something in your performance that is standing in your way. Hearing a specific complaint will allow you to answer it if it is false or correct it if it is true. It will also serve as a basis in future negotiations should you fail this time. "Last time you said my sales were down; well, I have increased them 23 percent since we last talked." If the company isn't doing well enough though you are, this may be the moment to point out the poor business practice of not rewarding hard and effective workers like you, who indeed are the corporation's hope for the future. Once again, ask if the two of you together can develop new ways to get your boss the happy hard worker desired while you get the money you want and need.

End Tactics

11. **Let the boss save face.** You cannot leave your superior with the feeling that you have won by intimidation or by forcing him or her to back down. If your manager cannot afford to lose you just before the busy season and feels deeply resentful at your opportunistic trading on this fact, deep scars will remain. Try to smooth over your victory and speak of it in terms of fairness to both of you. Let your superior know that you intend to give him or her what he or she paid for: loyal hard work and good value for the organization.

12. **Be slow to make concessions.** Although this point is implied in such techniques as silence, repetition, and saying no, it deserves to be discussed separately. When your superior refuses to give you more than a token raise that you consider completely inadequate, and gives as a reason some defect in your performance or in the company's, acknowledge the problem: "I admit I am a bit disorganized in my detail work, but in the bigger picture I was able to increase my calls on customers by 14 percent in the first three months," or "I know profits were down 3 percent for the corporation this past quarter, but in our department sales were up 9 percent." Don't fold and agree that this is not the time to seek a raise. Being slow to make concessions gives you time to pull yourself together when you feel attacked and may wear down your superior's resolve a bit.

13. **Close the deal.** Your goal (and your superior's) should be to get an agreement as quickly as possible, thus avoiding the danger of long-term struggles, ambiguities, and lingering hard feelings. Ask for any objections to your salary figure, overcome them or scale down the amount a bit, and once agreement is reached say "We agree then on an 18 percent raise" to close

the negotiation. If your boss remains firm and says absolutely not, attempt to delay his or her final decision and go through the procedure again until you can close the deal.

14. **Use other offers.** Sometimes they drop into your lap, but mostly you have to seek them out. Other people do not realize that most offers would be better termed requests. The statement "I have been approached about a vice-presidency at the Chemical Bank" usually means that you have turned over every stone, called in every favor, and pulled out all the stops to get a vice-presidency at the Chemical Bank. Seeking out other offers is very useful to your career for several reasons. Not only does it give you concrete evidence of what you are worth in the marketplace; it provides practice in interviewing, a chance to update your résumé, and proof that you are of worth to another company. It dispels fears that you'd better stay where you are because you are too old, too rusty, or too lazy, or because you fit so uniquely into your own job that you are of no use elsewhere.

Not only does a good offer do wonders for you, it wakes up your boss and the organization. If someone else thinks you're that good, you must be. Perhaps management has been taking your hard work for granted. It also opens the coffers very effectively. Many longtime employees feel very resentful when some new hotshot is hired at what seems a huge and disproportionate salary. The reason companies bid so high is to get the new person in the door. Why? For one, because the individual is new, a desirable stranger they want. But you have been there for five, ten, fifteen years. Why should they bid for your services? You are invested in the retirement plan, accustomed to the organization, and not threatening to leave. Imagine their surprise when you tell them of an offer for a better job at 20, 30, even 50 percent above what you are now earning.

The style with which you set off this bomb is essential to the relationship between you and your superior. You don't necessarily want him or her to say "We can't match that kind of money." Unless you simply wish to announce your departure, you value continuing positive feelings between you and your managers. Present your offer in a nonconfrontational manner. Say "I want to continue working for you and stay with this company, but I've been offered a job at 30 percent more than my present salary. I'm sure you understand how difficult it would be for me to leave, but I also know you realize that this is a great opportunity, and I feel my salary must be at market value."

You have clearly stated your request and listened carefully to your superior's objections, if any, and done your best to answer them through words and promised action. It is time to thank your superior for his or her time and attention. Encourage your boss to pursue your goals, and set a time for your next meeting.

Don't Be Surprised by Your Boss's Twenty-one Arguments

Somewhere in the discussion about your raise your boss will put forward one or more of twenty-one standard responses to stall and divert you. There are several reasons for this. One is that your manager is caught off guard and needs time both to feel out other concerned executives about your request and also to sort out his or her own feelings. A second is the hope that stalling you may make your request go away. Those in power are testing the seriousness of your commitment to get ahead and are making you nervous at the same time. The boss's ploys should be completely ignored by you psychologically and in negotiations must be quickly dismissed, while you continue your own pitch. The twenty-one answers fall into six categories and are easily recognized.

The Length-of-Service Arguments

1. **"It took me ten years to get my job and you've been here only a year and a half."**
2. **"People who have been here longer earn less."**

There are several ways to respond to these arguments, but it is essential that you dismiss them quickly and get back to the question of your own money needs. One simple answer is silence. This avoids discussing the diversion at all and may force your boss back to the subject. A second way is to handle the argument quickly in a subordinate clause and return to your main concern. You might briefly state that others who do good work should also be rewarded, or that ten years ago it may have taken a longer time to get a substantial raise but that is not the way things are now; then proceed with your review of your accomplishments. If you suspect that your boss really is afraid of a rebellion by other workers, you might acknowledge the fear briefly: "I don't blame you for being concerned about a deluge of raise requests, but this is not a question of all children being given the same allowance by their parents, but of a reward for work done and responsibility taken. The best should be paid well, and the rest can turn being upset about their lower wages into better performance." The essential point in all of these discussions is to terminate the discussion within a minute and return to the main issue. If your superior is anxious to continue the diversion, you will have to be firm, saying, "Managing the group is your job and I am sure a difficult one, but I am here to discuss my performance and my need for more money."

The Poorhouse Arguments

3. "We're having a terrible year."
4. "I'd like to help you but we must keep our overhead down."
5. "The budget won't permit it."
6. "The economy looks very bad."
7. "I can't even get myself a raise. How can I get you one?"
8. "This is a nonprofit organization."

It pays to have read the company's financial report. If times are not tough, then simply say so and return to your point. If they are tough, agree with your superior that business is slow and that the company needs to be careful with money, but that using it to motivate those who are the best bet to turn things around is using it wisely. A company must invest to make money, and one of the best investments is in its personnel. One interesting technique is to act surprised at how bad things are and say, "I didn't realize things were so tough," in an effort to get your superior to back down out of fear that he or she will start a rumor of impending bankruptcy. If you are truly convinced that your corporation is moribund, look for a new job immediately. Otherwise, bring a halt to this poor-mouthing and get back to discussing your raise.

The Personal-Need Arguments

9. "You don't need the money; you are a two-career family."
10. "You're single. You don't have a family to support."
11. "You want to buy another car!" "You're going to Europe twice this year!"
12. "You're never satisfied. You've gotten two raises in the last twenty-three months."

These are clearly diversions. Your marital status or how much your spouse earns is not the issue. The issue is how well you do your job, your value to the company, and whether your salary reflects your worth. Dismiss these arguments with such comments as: "My spouse's salary is not the issue"; "I'm single but my salary should not be based on my marital status but on . . ."; "I love my new car [or I enjoyed my vacation enormously] but here is why I think I should earn more money . . ."; or "Yes, I appreciate the two raises I've already received, but I started with a low salary and my responsibilities have been growing rapidly. Here is why I believe I deserve more money . . ." In each case, after the rapid preamble, go on to enumerate your accomplishments and your need for more money.

The Vague Performance Arguments

13. "You don't have enough experience."
14. "I'm not sure you're ready yet."
15. "You make a lot of mistakes."

Question your superior's estimate of your performance to see if it is a vague gambit or real. If it is a diversion, quickly dismiss it with "Yes, I am not all that senior, but here are my accomplishments and my increasing responsibilities, and the reason I want a raise is that there are people who do what I do who earn a lot more." If the mistakes are specific, admit them and show how your accomplishments far outweigh them. You don't have to be perfect to get a raise, just valuable to the company and worth more money.

The Comparison Arguments

16. **"Other employees aren't making that much."**
17. **"Many people would love to have your job."**
18. **"It's a lot more than what you've been making."**

Do not argue with your boss. If his assertion is reasonable, agree with it quickly and get back to your need for a raise. Without disparaging other employees, you might either ignore the comment about their earning less or agree that it is true, but reiterate that for the scope of your job you are indeed being underpaid. Your superior may say that many want your job, but remember he or she does not want to cope with losing you and breaking in another. You can acknowledge that your job is indeed desirable, but go on to show why you deserve more money. If what you are asking for is a lot more than you are making, emphasize that you have been underpaid and are worth the difference.

The Stalls

19. "I don't know, I'll have to talk to Sam about it."
20. "We're just reviewing salaries. I'll get back to you."
21. "I'll take it up at our next meeting."

Offer to prepare a memorandum listing your accomplishments for your boss to show Sam, or volunteer to go with your boss to present your case. Make your boss your ally as the two of you seek a raise for you. If your manager says he or she plans to take it up at the next meeting, find out when it is and get back to him or her promptly. This is a way to remind your supervisor that you are serious. Don't be put off if your boss hasn't gotten to it yet. Remind him or her how important it is to you, and check back until you get an answer.

There is no reason for your manager to stick to one set of reasons to distract you from your efforts. Be persistent and don't let him or her wear you down. If your supervisor disputes your assertion that you are performing at a higher level than you are being paid for, give him or her an example of some new function you are performing. If you've located a new supplier whose work is every bit as good as the present one but at half the price, tell him or her about it. If the manager implies good things in the vague future, get the discussion back to the subject of your present needs.

Consider the Personality Type
of Your Boss

You are positioned for a raise and have planned your negotiating tactics for the moment itself. Most books on negotiation recommend that you become a machine and deal with your boss as though he or she were one, too. If such volumes consider emotions at all, they do so superficially and suggest that you sit patiently and allow the other side to ventilate anger and blow off steam so they will feel better. But more subtle psychological issues are ignored. This is a serious error and can result in total disaster for you. It's like dancing only one step no matter what the music. Bosses differ, and you can handle them best if you understand the personality of the one with whom you are dealing.

We are really looking at two levels of negotiation. The first is the surface one outlined in most standard business books on the subject. This describes the rules of the game, the arena in which the struggle takes place. Participants are advised to focus on the issues, not the people, to search for areas favorable to both sides, and to employ fair and objective standards wherever possible rather than submit to the will of one side or the other. Emotions are viewed as interference, as something to be tolerated in one's opponent and controlled in oneself.

But underneath this is another level of negotiation that is much deeper and more complicated. And it is here that the battle is won or lost. In earlier sections I have focused on self-analysis and tried to help you discover what it is in you that prevents you from getting a raise. For example, if you view your boss as a major power and yourself as powerless, it is wise to begin to regard yourself as an adult and an equal. But the personality type of your superior strongly influences his or her bargaining style. The more you understand not only yourself but the kind of person or people you are up against, the better you will do. What follows are fifteen personality types you may meet on the day you ask for a raise. Stop and think which type (most are a combination of types) your boss is and you will find yourself much better prepared to win the raise you deserve.

The Narcissistic Boss

The Problem. The narcissistic boss is smooth, effective, and socially adept, but not so far beneath the surface lurks an excessively self-absorbed person, ambitious, grandiose, and overly dependent on external admiration and acclaim. Such a person has serious deficiencies in his or her capacity to love and be concerned about others; he or she lacks the capacity for empathy and consciously or unconsciously exploits others in a ruthless way. Egocentric bosses are envious and often lack impulse control or the capacity to tolerate anxiety.

Because this supervisor possesses a grandiose sense of self-importance and believes that you are "lucky to work for me," he or she feels entitled to your loyalty and hard work and to anything you might contribute to his or her success, power, or image of brilliance. When such an individual is criticized or feels threatened or slighted, he or she reacts with rage, shame, humiliation, and emptiness because of an excessive dependence on the admiration of others.

The Solution. The first way to handle such people is not to threaten them in any way but to show how you enhance their career and prestige: "Here is how I have helped and will help your success." Go on to show how their department will grow, the company will expand, sales will soar, and the successes will win them fame and honor. Flatter such executives by telling them what a good job they are doing and how much you will do for them. Only then should you ask for an increase in compensation, not so much for how good you are as for how good you make the boss look. One difficulty in dealing with such people is how angry they make you, because as you feed their egos, they in turn belittle your efforts, by comments such as that your role in the corporation is small. Do not defend yourself at such times but admit that "compared to your achievements mine are indeed small, but having helped you achieve a 23 percent increase in new orders over the past year, I think I deserve a 20 percent raise in salary."

The Dependent, Needy, Hypersensitive Boss

The Problem. These managers are submissive and ingratiating in order to gain approval; they are unable to assert their own views, wishes, or feelings. They passively allow others to make decisions, and tolerate abusive superiors and subordinates. These people are overly conscientious, perfectionistic, timid, shy, lacking in self-confidence, and afraid of friction or rebuffs.

The Solution. You must take charge of and for this superior without being too threatening. Fighting with his or her boss for your raise is totally beyond this submissive and ingratiating individual. He or she could barely battle for his or her own raise. Overcome your superior's fear of going to the organization for you by calming him or her. If this does not succeed, you may have to make a worse threat: for example, "I enjoy working for you and making a contribution to this company, but I can't stay if I'm not being paid my market value." Some dependent bosses can't be asked nicely, since their desire to please those above them is greater than the wish to do your bidding. Thus, you may have to be firm almost to the point of being abusive in order to get them to move on your request. This, of course, is a last resort, and sometimes it is possible to lead such a manager by showing him or her what to say and do. Occasionally he may agree that you may go to his boss alone or that you may go together, but you will have to speak for yourself while your boss smiles and risks nothing.

The Critical and Perfectionistic Boss

The Problem. Individuals who are perfectionistic are unable to satisfy themselves, so your chances of being appreciated for what to them are your careless and sloppy ways are virtually non-existent. Managers of this type are serious, formal, conventional, and stingy. They are excessively devoted to work, to the exclusion of pleasure and people. They find it hard to praise or to express warmth and tenderness. Scrooge is the caricature of such a boss. Real bosses of this type are more difficult to recognize and handle.

This kind of boss aggravates your own insecurities (we all have some, no matter how long we've been in therapy or how many self-help books we've read) because they spot your weaknesses and dwell on them. You may have streamlined the whole department so that it is twice as efficient as before, yet they spot only the remaining waste. They expect you to be as obsessed with details as they are and preoccupied with work to the exclusion of all else. If they don't make you nervous and insecure, their lack of support and appreciation can make you angry with them. Taking your good work for granted, they annoy you with their constant recitations of petty omissions.

Another of the many problems with such bosses is that no

matter how much salary research you do to discover your objective, fair market value, the exact percentage of your raise cannot be precisely determined scientifically, and ambiguity is very difficult for petty minds of this type. In addition, they are stingy and ungiving. They find it virtually impossible to reward you for what may have taken them fourteen years of laborious pettiness to achieve.

The Solution. Psychoanalysts find people of this type extremely difficult to budge even after years of treatment, so your task is not an easy one. It is to your advantage, however, to give it a clear, hard try. If you fail, you will have to find a way to get away from such a person, either by transferring to another department in your own firm or by changing companies altogether. There are two strategies you should try. First, be obsessive in your detail. Before the meeting, deliver a long, meticulous memo enumerating all your accomplishments since your last raise discussion. Do not name the sum you want on paper, but include everything else. At the meeting itself, if you bump into the expected resistance to your request because you failed to do some petty thing, do not defend that. Agree that it was indeed an oversight and return quickly to your achievements and salary requirements. Do not get mired down in detail with such a person, or you will never emerge from it.

If this strategy is not successful, you may as well try one a bit more risky. The next step is to frighten such a boss. Of course, it is best, as in all cases, to have a transfer within the company or a new job staked out before you try this maneuver. You might speak of the importance of giving a worker incentive to get ahead and suggest that your supervisor has not thought of this aspect of his or her job. You may have to raise the ante to "I can't stay here if I am not rewarded. During my last year here not only have I mastered the complexity of my job so that it runs smoothly, but I have expanded my responsibilities to include purchasing and the new method of record keeping. It would take a new person six months to master the system." You have thus threatened your superior not only with leaving but with six months of training your successor and potential chaos. Petty people do not like change or disorder, and your trump card may indeed work.

The Depressive Boss

The Problem. Overseers like these feel hopeless and helpless. Their depression saps their strength, and any request out of the ordinary seems like the last straw added to their already unbearable burden. The black mood colors everything: their view of the company's potential, the business climate, and their future and yours. They try to inflict their lack of hope on you.

Your request for a raise is a problem for them that they wish would go away. They will show no enthusiasm at your meeting, and you will feel unsupported. Some depressives are irritable and when you request a raise will snap: "You just got one!" or "The company cannot afford it." The latter is not a ploy. They really do think everything is bad and that the company is going down the drain, taking them along. Other depressives are stone-faced to the point where you may feel they don't like you. Sometimes you may be right, in that they envy what they see as your happy life, filled with friends and interests they don't believe exist in theirs. Or you may misinterpret their fixed stare as disapproval when it has nothing to do with you at all. Any insecurities you have will be magnified.

The Solution. The degree of depression is a key element. If it is too severe, no one can reach this person, let alone get him or her to agree to a raise. It must be recognized that depression is different from a bad mood and getting the boss on the wrong day. It is a fixed condition lasting weeks or months. In some cases it becomes chronic and influences the supervisor's character subtly and lastingly. This is the kind of person who is always pessimistic and tends to be rigid, because any change is a threat to the precarious balance of his or her mood.

One way to handle depressed bosses is to try to motivate them with your own enthusiasm, since they don't have any of their own. By providing energy and a format for them, you threaten their equilibrium only minimally. Such bosses are usually passive and will agree to your request in order to get the problem (your request) to go away. If your enthusiasm (low-key, please, around depressed people) does not do the trick, a combative approach may be effective. "If there is no hope for the company or my getting a raise, why should I stay here?" This forces the boss to confront his or her own negative outlook and may allow you to argue him or her out of it long enough to get a raise.

The Seductive Boss

The Problem. These supervisors come in two types—the personal and the business—although some combine both. The personal seducer makes you a friend, touches you, is warm and encouraging, and may or may not make sexual overtures. The erotic offer may be an expression of true love or an attempt to satisfy lust in an exercise of the power they have over your career. The linkage of the salary raise to the sexual favor ranges from the heavy-handed direct approach to subtle innuendo. Sometimes it is imagined, when the offer is in fact friendly and not physical. Like the erotic offer, the one for friendship may be sincere or manipulative, but in either case an employee may feel inhibited in requesting a raise in what seems to be a social rather than a business relationship. Some women fall into this trap with the older male boss who is like a kind father.

The second seductive type—the "business seducer"—is long on promises regarding your future but short on delivery. His style is warm and caring. He takes you to an expensive lunch on the company or gets you tickets for the World Series or a play, but is very slow to reward you with money. He tells you, "You are doing a wonderful job and will have a long and successful career with this organization." Such bosses are easy to like because they know how to motivate you and make you feel appreciated.

The Solution. The personal sexual seducers need to have their hands pushed aside as you quietly say that you are not available because of your husband or your boyfriend or girlfriend. Don't throw a tantrum or humiliate your superior if you can handle the situation in a low-key fashion. Your feeling of "how dare you" should be set aside in favor of effectively stopping the action without damaging your relationship with the person too much. If your quiet effort fails, you will have to raise the decibel level a bit, saying "I'm sure you didn't mean to make a pass at one of your employees," and if this does not work you may have to threaten to report your superior and then do it.

The boss who seems to want to be your friend may truly wish to have a more than professional relationship with you, because of either loneliness or pleasure in your company. The old adage about not mixing business with pleasure usually holds, and it is best to refuse while avoiding insulting your superior. Getting raises and promotions is usually accomplished best in a professional atmosphere, but there are exceptions. You and your superior may be able to have some social relationship outside of work, but carefully and without too much intensity. Otherwise, the ups and downs of the emotions may color your work association. You don't want your manager to be angry with you because you omitted his or her name from your guest list one evening.

Finally, the boss who pretends to be your friend in order to manipulate you better must be detected and dealt with firmly but calmly. Since sincerity is sometimes hard to distinguish from dishonesty, this is another reason to be careful about too much socializing with your superior.

Business seducers give pats on the back (not the behind) and lots of praise, but nothing concrete. It is essential that you recognize how much you like working for this appreciative person who promises you a bright and glorious future. The most extreme example of this I ran into personally was when applying for a job at a very fine Catholic hospital. When it came time to talk salary the head psychiatrist told me that the institution tended to believe its physicians would be rewarded in the next life. You, too, may have to wait that long unless you hold your ground and create a time framework. "I need this title and money and must have an answer within the next two weeks. I need to see movement in my career. I enjoy working for you. I like you and my job, but I need a raise [name the amount] and a promotion, and I must have an answer."

The Authoritarian Boss

The Problem. Such bosses are cold, aloof, arrogant, and controlling. They do not see their working with you as a collaboration between equal adults, but as one in which they have the power and you are to obey. They want things their way and are prone to say such things as "We just don't consider raises around here midyear" and "There just isn't any money for raises now." They present themselves as the ones who know reality and set the rules unilaterally. Workers who had such parents or who don't want to take too much responsibility do well under such bosses, but most Americans don't like dictators and find such bosses insufferable.

The Solution. If you can stand them, accept these authoritarian qualities in the everyday work world and do not try to fight them. In the meeting about your raise, however, it is wise to ignore the initial "definite" no. Appeal to your boss as an authority figure by saying "You're in charge of my career. I've made a contribution to this organization and need to be compensated for it." Authoritarian types who stand by themselves on pinnacles tend to be lonely and may respond to your description of how much you've learned from them, how valuable you have found their guidance, and how much you would miss them if you could no longer work for them. Do not, however, threaten to quit directly. Rather, attempt through your almost obsequious flattery to disarm this person whom everyone else hates and avoids. "I want to stay here and work with you. I admire your ability to make decisions quickly and unemotionally, but I need a more definite idea of my future."

The Jealous and Envious Boss

The Problem. Managers like these think you now have too much and are disinclined to reward you with more. Since they perceive you as having beauty, social status, ability, money, and the affection of co-workers, they would like to see you fail where they have control. Many employees are not fully aware when their boss is envious and regards the underling as better off. Focused on your own money problems, you may not realize that your manager regards you as lucky because you are young, attractive, and well liked. Such managers feel that they are less well off than you are and don't want to increase what they already view as a disparity.

Bosses of this type also do not understand that having the best people working for them enhances their reputation. Instead, they are threatened by your ability rather than realizing how your addition to the group improves their position with those above them.

The Solution. Keep a low profile with such managers. Don't flaunt your physical, intellectual, social, or financial assets in front of them. Then, make them feel that they are an extremely important part of your work life. Make them aware of how they have helped your success, and be effusive in your credit. Ask for advice and direction even if you don't need it. This is an effective way to make your superior feel powerful and competent. Test these methods over a period of several weeks to a month to determine whether your superior can bear your getting ahead or is so envious that he or she is determined to prevent it. In the latter instance you'd better go around or away from this individual.

The Chauvinistic Boss

The Problem. The chauvinist is a common character in the corporate structure. He sees women as mothers, wives, daughters, or lovers, but not as equal and respected colleagues. This executive may be of any personality type (for example, seducer, jealous and envious, threatened, authoritarian). His problem may be complemented by the woman employee who enjoys the role of mother, wife, daughter, or lover, and neglects her rights as an equal and a wage earner. She may become too loyal to the male chauvinist, thus secretly damaging her chances for a raise. Once a company senses that they have you captive, they have little or no motivation to bid up your salary.

The Solution. Emphasize your professionalism and be reluctant to discuss your personal life or to reveal any of the nonbusiness roles into which the dominant male tries to fit you. Apply steady, nonaggressive pressure in your attempt to be equal and businesslike. Ask to be called by your surname if it is customary for others on your level. Don't wear little-girl or maternal clothes. Inquire a little less after your boss's health and the state of his family and more about sales and when the new shipment will arrive.

In your actual raise discussion, parry your superior's remarks about how you don't need more money because you will "go off and get married" or because "you have a husband who supports you" or because "you'll leave soon to have children" with calm answers about how "women are as loyal as men, and men leave jobs, too." Remind him that the subject is not your private life but adequate compensation for your level of responsibility and performance. Such talk will go far to increase his respect for your professionalism and discourage him from continuing to regard you as his girl.

The Emotional Boss

The Problem. Emotional executives are volatile, inconsistent, dramatic, and disorganized. They tend to exaggerate and overreact, may have irrational outbursts and tantrums, and love the spotlight. The effect on their employees is unsettling, as one moment they are kind and supportive, the next moody and nasty. You don't know what to expect and are constantly off balance, fearful of their tantrums, irritated by their unwillingness to give credit as they greedily take it all, and confused by a mixture of feelings toward them because they are so nice one minute and so mean the next. These superiors are among the worst, because you don't know what you are dealing with from one moment to the next.

The Solution. The first step is to try to limit the boss's range. Gently try to arrive at some objective policy and a standard of behavior less susceptible to mood changes. Obviously, this is easier said than accomplished and runs the risk of inciting the superior to further fury. Next, don't be upset by outbursts or take them personally. It is easy to see that this executive acts that way with everyone. And stop being surprised by the volatility; it is predictable.

Get the boss to listen to you. Pick your time for the salary review carefully and try for one of relative calm if that is possible. Submit your request in writing a few days ahead so that your emotional superior can scrutinize it calmly when alone. Make yourself essential to this disorganized victim of excessive emotions by creating order for him or her. Become the problem solver at times of real or emotional emergency. "Let me take care of that for you," you say to your distraught superior. Then you might add, "Now that I've solved your problem, I need you to focus on mine."

Highly emotional superiors are too buffeted about by their own psychological changes to focus long enough to successfully get a raise for you. There are two effective and, oddly, opposite ways to get their attention. One is to make a big noise, in fact a scene, and the other is by extreme stillness and calm. You may have to emotionally exaggerate your needs in order to be heard, or be as dramatic as your manager. Some people don't hear words, only shouts. Or in a hushed voice you may show you mean business as you carefully enunciate how "I need to talk to you about my career. We should get together when there are no interruptions. I have to have a raise and a promotion and must have an answer in a week, at which time I'll talk to you to see what management said about it.''

The Guarded and Secretive Boss

The Problem. Executives of this kind are terrified about being scrutinized themselves by those above them. The raise process opens up the issue of profitability to others. Can the organization afford to pay you more? What has its performance been like recently? How is the whole department doing? The boss who is socially phobic, guarded, or secretive does not want an emotional interchange with his or her employer. The salary meeting is a potentially charged one, a threat to the quiet, control, and anonymity the superior seeks. It could be a source of humiliation or embarrassment.

The Solution. Such people must be approached in a low-key and careful way. They must be reassured that the department—*their* department—is strong enough to afford to pay you more money. It can be extremely effective, should simple reassurance fail, to replace the boss's fear of being scrutinized by another one he or she has overlooked. This will surprise and perhaps budge him or her. Thus, you should point out that ''upper management may be wondering why this department does not promote or give raises and might be concerned about how you are bringing your people along. An endorsement from you and the firm will make others feel that this department is a training ground for future management, and I think I deserve a raise because . . .''

The Passive-Aggressive Boss

The Problem. These supervisors resist demands for performance indirectly, rather than by directly refusing. They procrastinate, dawdle, are stubborn, intentionally inefficient, and conveniently forgetful. They are the postal clerk or the person at the Bureau of Motor Vehicles who will not move the slightest bit faster no matter how long the line.

The Solution. These people can be very hard to move. The harder you press, the more stubbornly slow they can become. As in all negotiations, you should try to set a brief time so as to get it over quickly before either side has a chance to become wedded to a particularly resistant stance. One essential and effective way is not to set yourself against such bosses but to align yourself with them in your effort to get to upper management on your behalf. Be as helpful as you can be, offering a memo outlining your accomplishments over the last year for them to take to upper management. If you hear nothing, tell them you will speak to them in a week and *keep doing so.* Passive-aggressives thrive on tiring people out, so be prepared to outlast them. "I know how busy you are," you might say, "but I wonder if you've reached a decision on my request for a higher salary."

The Blaming Boss

The Problem. Bosses like these avoid responsibility even when it is clearly theirs. Such individuals may also be narcissistic, fearful, insecure, passive-aggressive, or emotional. Even though this overlap coexists with other personality types, it is included as a separate category because this attribute stands out so significantly and is the predominant factor influencing dealings with such a person. Bosses like these consciously and/or unconsciously attribute both their problems and those of the organization to you and perhaps others. Because of this, they are prone to believe you do not deserve a raise.

The Solution. Parry with bosses of this type who say "you don't deserve a raise" by saying "Look at what happened to sales last month" or "True, sales are down, but here is what I've done about turning things around in the fall" or "Look how I've reduced overhead." Try to discover why they don't want to give you a raise: "If there is a reason you don't feel I deserve more money, would you please tell me so that I can correct the fault." The blamer may begin to realize that his or her criticism is not specifically of you but is a general feeling. Disengage yourself from the blamer's charges that are not your fault; admit, deal with, and correct those weaknesses that really describe you; and return to a description of your performance and responsibilities and why it entitles you to a raise.

The Indecisive Boss

The Problem. We all know people who cannot make decisions because they fear making the wrong one or because they cannot bear closing off an option. Some are dependent and look for others to decide for them, and others will take advice from no one. Whatever is behind your boss's inability to make choices, it can hurt your career: not only might he or she block your raise attempts, but your efforts in general run into this wall of jelly when you most need backing and support.

The Solution. Usually such bosses are not mean and deliberately holding you back. Often they will respond when given a strong and organized argument for why you need more money.

The key is to run things for such an individual. If he or she is the worst type—one who won't run things and won't let you do so either—then you will have to leave. Make your case, try to get your boss to agree on the spot, and lead your superior. Often it will work.

The Anxious and Threatened Boss

The Problem. These people worry constantly, anticipate misfortune, and feel threatened by everything and everyone. They can be immobilized by their fear of those above and threatened by those below.

The Solution. Try to calm them by reassuring them that the worst won't happen. Don't threaten them, since they will only become more defensive. Remind them that your success is their success, that you are with and for them. You are loyal, respect them, understand their problem, and consider yourself part of the solution. Here is what you have done to help them and what you intend to do in the future, and that is why you deserve a raise.

The Fair Boss

The Problem. Bosses like these are all any of us could want. Secure and humane, they want to motivate, help, and get the best out of you. They encourage free exchange and expect to give an honest appraisal of your strengths and weaknesses. They welcome suggestions and comments, even if they don't like what they hear. They are willing to teach you and to learn from you. Giving credit does not threaten them. Such bosses can be tough negotiators.

The Solution. Because they are not neurotically needy, susceptible to flattery, or excessively fearful of losing you, the deal you work is likely to be close to your true worth. If your self-esteem is low, you may not get much of a raise from them, and if your performance is under par the money will not be forthcoming. But if you have been carefully attending your career in preparation for your money talk, you have nothing to fear from such a boss.

After you get your raise, which you may not find completely satisfactory, you must begin to position yourself for the future. It takes time to build your case for advancement and a raise.

Getting ahead takes more than brains, initiative, and hard work; it takes the ability to get along with people. It takes a great deal of self-analysis, the capacity to view others unemotionally, and self-control. You really have two jobs, your everyday work plus the thoughtful and effective planning of your future. No one else will take charge of your situation. It's up to you to manage your career in a way that will make you feel challenged by and satisfied in your work life.

Index